I0411850

TABLE OF CONTENTS

LIST OF FIGURES

I. INTRODUCTION

Purpose

The purpose of this paper is to describe the threat posed by Islamic extremist movements to the United States. Recent unsettling events have focussed America's attention to the potential threat presented by countries and movements dominated by the radical version of the Islamic religion. These events include the 1979 hostage taking at the American embassy in Tehran, the 1983 bombing of the U.S. embassy in Beirut, the 1983 bombing of the Marine headquarters in Beirut, the kidnapping of American citizens during the 1980s which resulted in the brutal murders of two of the hostages, the 1985 hijacking of TWA flight 847 and murder of a U.S. serviceman aboard, Desert Storm, and the 1993 World Trade Center bombing.

A wide range of opinions exists as to the type of threat posed by these movements. The spectrum of opinions ranges from a monolithic, well organized, multinational movement centrally directed from Iran to an unorganized group of movements whose cooperation is coincidental and has no common goal or direction. The following qu9tes support the argument of a monolithic movement.

> "... well coordinated campaign originating in Iran and aided by Sudan ... spearheaded by extremists groups engaged in terrorism and other violence, such as Hamas and Hezbollah."[1]

"Iran is the center of the world's new Comintern ... The ultimate aim is a united Islamic front to confront Western arrogance. The immediate aim is to destroy pro-Western regimes, to seize the Gulf and its weak oil-rich sheikdoms, and to eradicate that singular affront to Islam: Israel."[2]

"... Sudan emerged as an Iranian strategic outpost and key infrastructure for the export of the Islamic revolution throughout the Near East and Africa. Khartoum is committed to its role in Tehran's grand design."[3]

The opposing argument of a disorganized group of independent movements with minimal cooperation and no internationally centralized direction is expressed in the quotes below.

"... loose assemblage of groups with more or less common goals but dramatically different strategies that depend on local conditions. There is no Islamic international orchestrating revolutionary acts of terror and bloodshed around the world."[4]

"Most students do not accept the claim of a cohesive, transnational Islamist movement led by Iran."[5]

"There is no single worldwide Islamic resurgence ... not members of a single group or nation; their tactics and intensity are as diverse as their backgrounds."[6]

To determine the extent of the threat posed by Islamic extremists to U.S. national interests - supply of Persian Gulf oil, access to seaways, and survival of regional allies - it is necessary to determine the degree of cooperation between regimes and movements an the amount of direction provided by the Islamic Republic of Iran. This paper will show that the various Islamic extremist movements are well organized, share networks, and cooperate to achieve common goals.

Almost every century has witnessed bursts of Islamic violence - violence sponsored or carried out directly or indirectly by groups espousing Islam - since the founding of the religion. Three key events occurred in the last fifteen years which have combined to present the world with the current threat of renewed violence. The first event was Ayatollah Khomeini's success in gaining power in Iran in 1979. The forces of Khomeini were aided by the Palestinian Liberation Organization (PLO) and other radical Palestinian groups with the support of Syria during the 1970s.

The second event that had a great effect upon the Islamic extremist movement also occurred in 1979 - the Soviet Union's invasion of Afghanistan. The invasion triggered an onslaught of Moslem volunteers from throughout the world, primarily from the Middle East, to aid their Moslem brethren in repelling the "infidels". As the conflict drew to an end and the Soviets withdrew, the Arab veterans returned to their homes and became leaders and foot soldiers of a new holy war against the moderate secular regimes in their native lands.

The third key event was the 1989 coup d'etat in Sudan that left the largest country in Africa with an extremist Islamic regime. This ruthless regime is waging a civil war against the African, Christian, and animist minority in the south of the country. They are also engaging in ethnic cleansing against African minorities and human rights abuses in denying food to the starving population in the rebellious south.

Sudan has signed treaties with Iran and is suspected of being the conduit of extremists returning from Afghanistan to their native lands throughout the Middle East. Iran is accused of supplying funding and training to various extremist groups that attend training camps in Sudan. These groups come from countries throughout North Africa, Palestine, the Arabian Peninsula, Central Asia, and East Africa. Finally, recent acts and planned acts of terrorism in the U.S. point to the possible involvement of Sudan and Iran. An analysis of this international Islamic extremist network reveals cooperation between the three regimes to achieve their common goals and support for other Islamic extremist groups.

Defining Extremism

Establishing a definition for extremism is the first step in understanding the threat that may be posed by it. Extremism is a political phenomenon involving acts of excess and violence by individuals and groups who espouse a particular ideology. To fully understand Islamic extremism, it is necessary to briefly describe some aspects of Islam and contrast the terms Islamic fundamentalism, political Islam, and Islamic extremism.

The brutal acts of violence, terrorism, and martyrdom are the portrayal of Islam that is often presented to the West. Islam is actually a religion that encourages virtues such as generosity, charity, compassion, reconciliation, and equality. Classical Islam is one of the most tolerant of the world's religions.[7] The virtuous basis of the Islamic religion is evident as Islamic philanthropic organizations throughout history have established hospitals, clinics, orphanages, and schools in poverty stricken areas throughout the Middle East.

The Western media have portrayed the militant side of Islam as a unique product of a particular sect, Shia Islam. This was an observation primarily derived from acts of violence by Shi'ites in Iran and the Hezbollah in Lebanon and elsewhere throughout the 1980s. Although Shia movements were at the forefront of extremist acts, it is incorrect to label the entire sect as militants. Many Shi'ites display the compassion and tolerance that are characteristic of the majority of the world's Moslems.

Until the establishment of an extremist regime in Sudan and the violent subversive movements throughout North Africa, the Sunni sect was reported as the compassionate and humanitarian branch, incapable of the violence of the Shi'ites. The West has been awakened to the threat presented by radical Sunni Moslems in the 1990s. Extremism is not the exclusive product of either sect, but a result of the manipulation of disenfranchised Moslems of both sects by radical leaders.

The Shia sect of Islam consists of only 10 percent of the world's Moslems. Over 50 percent of the world's Shia Moslems reside in Iran. The other principal concentrations are in the south of Iraq, Bahrain, Kuwait, the United Arab Emirates (UAE), the eastern province of Saudi Arabia, Lebanon, Syria, and Yemen.[8]

The division into the two major sects originated in the seventh century as a political dispute over the succession to the prophet Muhammed. The Sunni faction revolted against the ascension of Ali, the cousin and son-in-law of Muhammed, as the successor. This disagreement culminated when the Shi'ite followers of Ali, led by Ali's second son Hussain, were massacred by the Sunnis at Karbala in 680. From that time differences between the two sects were broadened to include ritual, legal, and theological matters.[9] The martyrdom of Hussain at Karbala is portrayed regularly by Shi'ites in passion plays. This tradition of martyrdom is one of the reasons for the assumption in the 1980s that violence and martyrdom were unique to the Shia.

The term Islamic fundamentalism has been incorrectly used to describe the various militant groups that use violent methods to address their worldly grievances, subvert secular Arab governments, engage in terrorism, and oppose the ongoing peace process. This descriptive term gives a misleading impression that all Moslems who strive to implement a "back-to-basics" religious practice are engaging in subversion and violent activities. The term Islamic fundamentalism is more appropriately applied to those movements who wish a revival of religious virtues or who want to return to the source of religious theology and knowledge. They feel that Islam has become corrupted and their redefining of the religion is a form of purging or redemption. Fundamentalism is a struggle between the forces of modernization and tradition. The fundamentalists do not necessarily reject modernization, especially when it improves living standards, but are opposed to the inevitable effect that modernization has on the erosion of traditions. Fundamentalists strive to make use of modernization to benefit the followers of their traditions, while shielding the same followers from the excesses of modernization. Islamic fundamentalists desire to see all or part of the following: the establishment of governments in accordance with the teachings of the Koran, application of the shari'a, or Islamic code of law, the application of Islamic principles in the economy, the removal of the corrupting influences of the West, a return of an Islamic community throughout the Middle East and North Africa, and a return to Islamic morals in their societies.[10] Islamic extremists often operate under the umbrella of the fundamentalist groups and many trace their origins to break-away movements from the fundamentalist groups. The majority of Moslems who are classified as fundamentalists are peace loving people who look upon the militant extremists as aberrations of their religion.

Another term that is frequently misused to describe the militant extremists is political Islam. Political Islam is a generic term referring to a conceptual framework involving the fusion of religion and politics to achieve a certain end: an Islamic government. This does not infer that an Islamic nation will be anti-Western or will be a pariah in world politics. Figure 1 provides examples of three types of political Islam.

The term Islamic extremism, Islamic militancy, or Islamist more accurately describes the potential threat that is examined in this paper. Islamic extremism is defined as unconventional

FUNDAMENTALIST STATES

(Islamic law for civil, criminal, and administrative issues)

                    Bahrain
                    Kuwait
                    Oman
                    Qatar
                    Saudi Arabia
                    United Arab Emirates

SECULAR STATES

(Islamic law for civil issues; secular law for criminal and
administrative issues)

                    Egypt
                    Iraq
                    Libya
                    Morocco
                    Pakistan
                    Syria
                    Tunisia

ISLAMIST STATES

(Islamic law for civil, criminal, and administrative issues;
state sponsorship of terrorism, aid to other extremists)

                    Iran
                    Sudan

Figure 1. Three Types of Political Islam

political participation involving one or more of the following:
1) terrorism, 2) non-tolerance, or 3) violent attacks against
civilian non-combatants. The Islamic extremist movements and
regimes often display all the characteristics of fundamentalism
and political Islam with the added factor of militancy, violence,

and terrorism to eradicate non-Moslem influences. One of the primary long term goals of the extremists is the reestablishment of the Islamic empire of the 1500s; Figure 2 indicates the extent of the empire. These movements are incited by the writings and teachings of radical Shia and Sunni clergymen, jurists, and political operatives such as the Ayatollah Khomeini, the

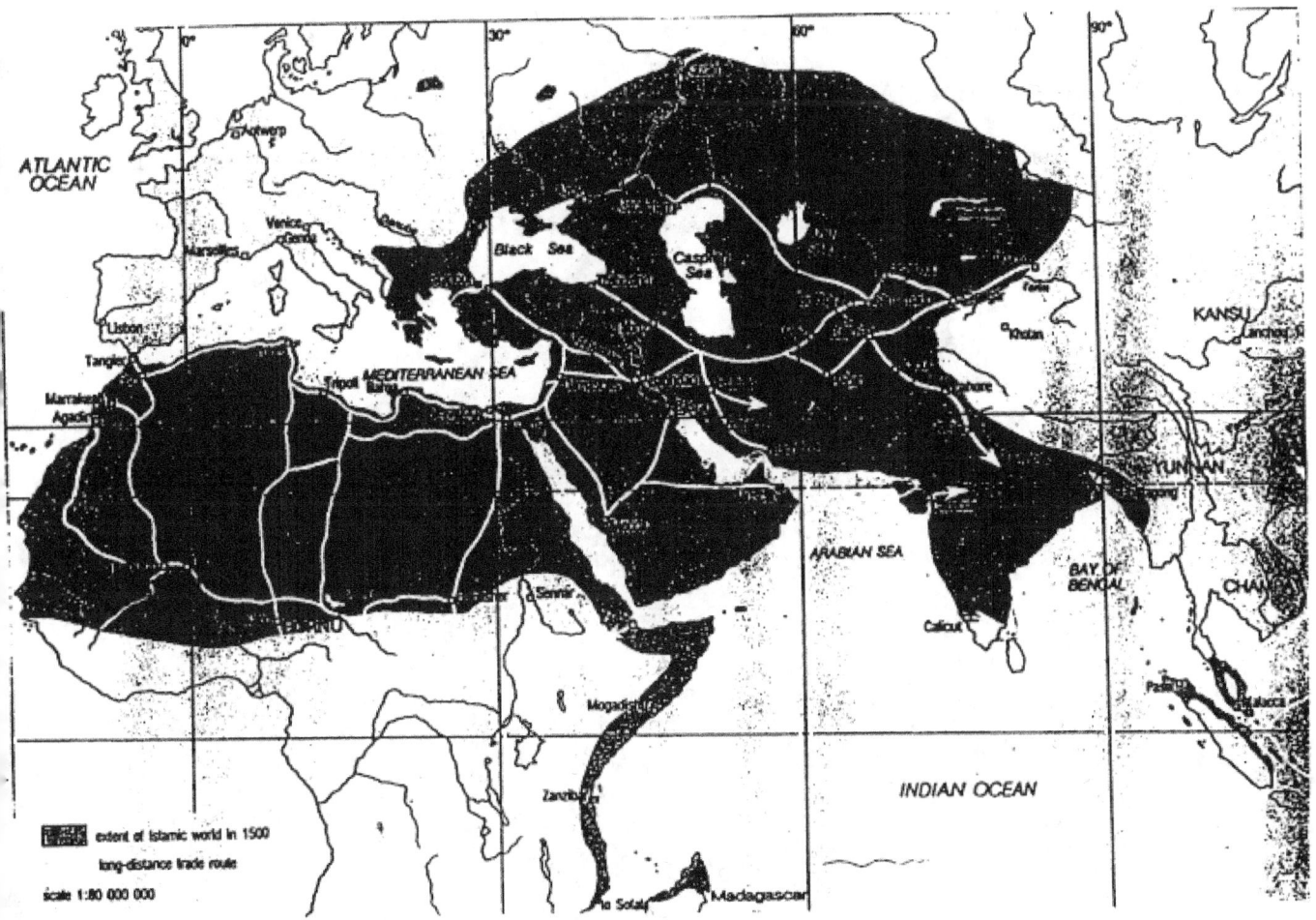

spiritual leader and founder of the Islamic Republic of Iran; Omar Abdel Rahman, the spiritual guide of Egypt's two main

Figure 2. Islamic Empire in 1500[14]

extremist groups, Gama'a and Al Jihad[11]; Muhammed Husayn
Fadlallah, the spiritual leader of Lebanon's Hezbollah[12]; Hassan
al-Turabi, the leader of Sudan's National Islamic Front (NIF)[13];
and many others.

U.S. National Interests

The anti-Western sentiment expressed by Islamic extremist
movements do not present a threat in and of themselves. To
determine if a threat exists to the United States, the extent of
impact upon national interests must be determined. The following
quotes from the 1993 Regional Defense Strategy broadly define
the goals of our national security interests:

> "National security interests can be translated into four
> mutually supportive strategic goals: ... goal is to
> preclude a hostile power from dominating a region critical
> to our interests ... These regions include ... the Middle
> East/Persian Gulf ... nondemocratic control of the
> resources of such a critical region could generate a
> significant threat to our security".[15]

> "In the Middle East and Persian Gulf, we should ...
> safeguard our access to international air and seaways and
> to the region's important source of oil. ... must be
> prepared 'to counter the terrorism, insurgency and
> subversion that adversaries may use to threaten governments
> supportive of U.S. security interests".[16]

From these quotes, clear national security interests are
identified. These include access to oil, access to air and
seaways, and threats to friendly governments in the region.
Additionally, key strategic minerals are produced in regions
adjacent to the Middle East. The spread of extremism may
endanger our access to these strategic minerals. This subject

will be addressed in more detail in the analysis of extremism's impact on East Africa and Central Asia.

Oil

The importance of oil in the U.S. economy is well known. The Middle East accounts for 45 percent of the world's oil and controls over 65 percent of the world's known oil reserves.[17] Figure 3 indicates the estimated oil reserves held by each country in the Middle East. Oil accounts for 40 percent of America's energy. Forty-five percent of this oil is imported. Twenty-five percent of the imports are from the Persian Gulf. Therefore, Persian Gulf oil accounts for less than five percent of America's energy consumption.[18] The question arises as to why

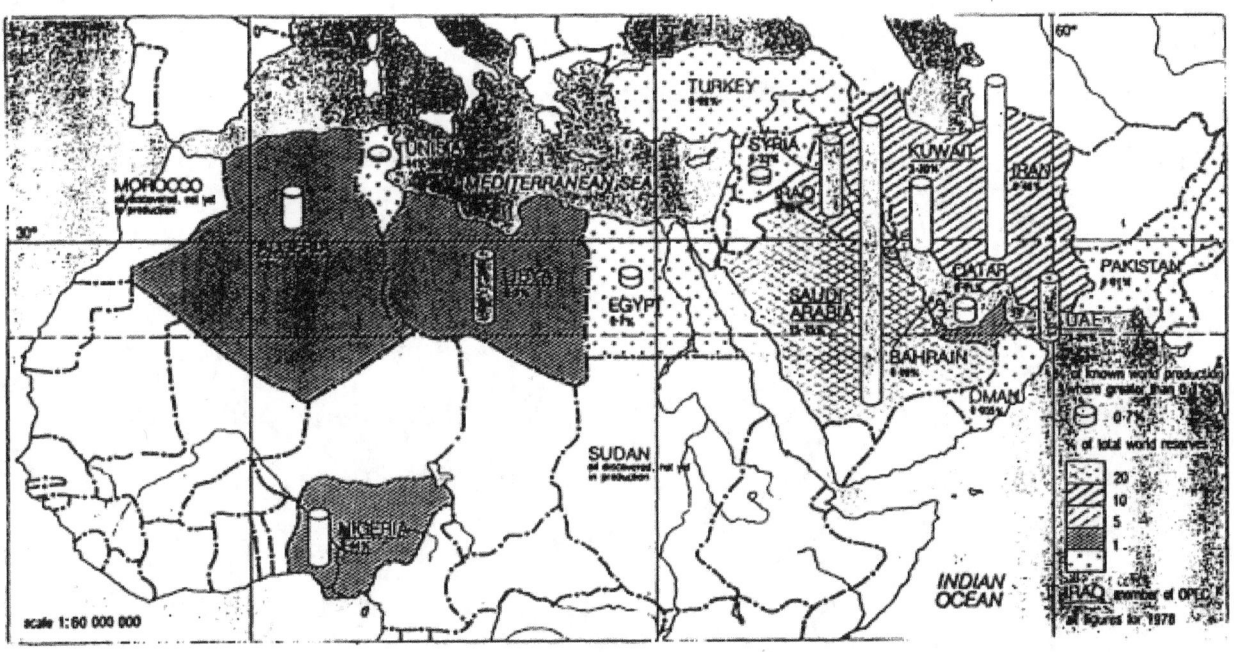

Figure 3. Distribution of Oil Reserves in the Middle East[19]

the United States should be concerned and devote so much
attention to access of Persian Gulf oil if our dependence on it
is so small.

Although the size of the oil reserves is a cause for
concern, the ease of access and low price of Persian Gulf oil
are equally important factors to draw our interest. The cost to
produce oil in the Persian Gulf is low relative to other
sources. The reserves are cheap and easy to tap.[20] The relative
low cost of the oil, combined with the fact the U.S. Department
of Energy forecasts that by the year 2010, our oil imports will
nearly double (from 45 to 72 percent), indicates that we will
become increasingly dependent on Persian Gulf oil.[21] The price of
oil will likely be kept low by the Gulf countries to ensure the
West remains interested and strategically involved in the Gulf.
The price of oil will be maintained at a level to make attempts
at developing alternative sources of energy economically
infeasible to the U.S..

A comparison of a few economies reveals the nature of the
West's dependence on Persian Gulf oil. The U.S. dependence is
less than 5 percent, Japan's is 37 percent, and Great Britain
imports no Persian Gulf oil.[22] Yet the U.S. and Great Britain
remain the most involved of the Western countries in the Gulf.
One of the primary reasons for this is the fungibility of oil; it
flows to the highest bidder. As long as the world depends upon
the Persian Gulf for one third of its oil, loss of this source of
oil will increase world prices and everyone, including the U.S.

and Great Britain, will pay more for imported oil. The higher prices will stimulate inflation and other related economic problems.[23]

The interdependence of the world economy also contributes to the importance of Gulf oil. As an example, foreign trade has tripled its share in the U.S. economy from 5 to 15 percent of Gross National Product (GNP). A third of the growth in the U.S. economy during the period 1986-1991 is attributable to exports.[24] As our economy becomes more interdependent with our industrialized allies, interruption in their oil supply will impact our economy. Figure 4 reveals the foreign energy

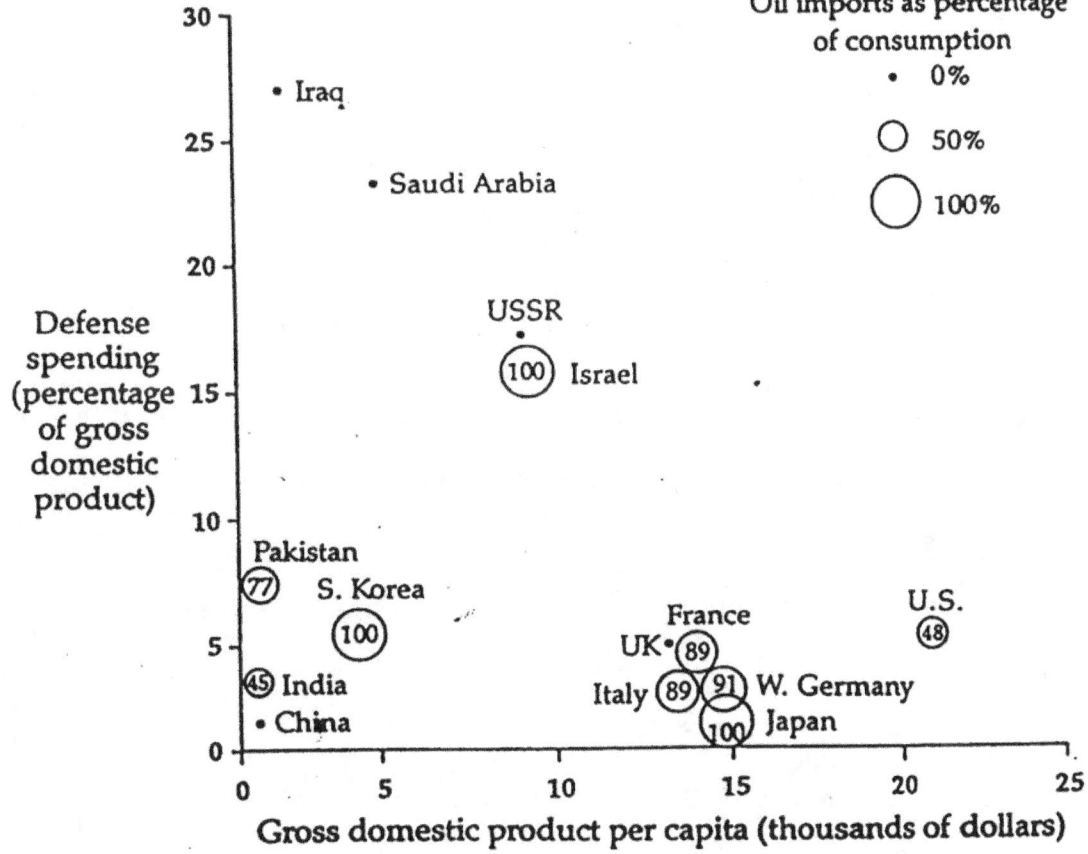

Figure 4. National Wealth, Defense Commitment, and Foreign Energy Dependence - 1990[25]

dependency, national wealth, and defense commitment of several
of our allies and opponents in 1990.

The Gulf states have become integral parts of the Western
financial system. In 1989 Kuwait earned more on investments in
the West than on oil production. Therefore any oil pricing
decisions made by the Gulf states must take into account the
impact on Western economies.[26]

Access to Seaways

The second aspect of the Middle East that merits attention
is the strategic chokepoints in the area. These chokepoints are
of vital interest to the world economy. Not only oil but 15
percent of all world commerce is routed through these. strategic
waterways.[27] These chokepoints include the Strait of Hormuz, the
entranceway to the Persian Gulf; the Bab el Mandeb, the
entranceway to the Red Sea; the Suez Canal; and the Strait of
Gibraltar. Any conflict that threatens to close these
chokepoints would have a drastic impact on the world's economy.[28]
The following sections detailing the threat from Iran and Sudan
will illuminate the dangers to these chokepoints.

Alliances

The third type of national interest that is at stake in the
Middle East is the threat to the allies of the U.S.. Our primary
allies in the region are Israel, Egypt, and the countries of the
Gulf Cooperation Council (GCC) - Saudi Arabia, Kuwait, Bahrain,
Qatar, the UAE, and Oman. Israel has been a steadfast ally of
the United States and a counterweight to the Soviet supported

states in the Middle East during the Cold War. The end of the Cold War has revealed little change in the U.S. view of the importance of Israel.

Egypt has been a cornerstone of U.S. policy in the Middle East. The main breakthrough in the Arab-Israeli conflict occurred in 1979 when Israel and Egypt signed a separate peace agreement. This bold event ensured Egypt would remain a key ally in U.S. Middle East strategy. Egypt's importance to the U.S. is apparent in the 2.2 billion dollars received each year from the U.S. in military and economic aid.[29] Egypt was among the first nations to provide troops to the U.S. led coalition for Operations Desert Shield and Desert Storm. Egypt's geographic importance lies in two factors: ownership of the Suez Canal and a common border with Israel.

Saudi Arabia and the other five members of the GCC are the remaining close allies of the U.S. in the region. In addition to the supply of oil, the GCC monarchies provide basing rights, host nation support, and participate in joint exercises, as well as maintain a pro-Western stance. Any threat to these nations would be seen as jeopardizing the supply of oil to the West.

II. THE THREAT

Overview

The Islamic extremist threat is centered around three regimes: Iran, Sudan, and the Islamic Party of Afghanistan, one of the major factions struggling for control of that nation. The threat is much broader than these three regimes, however it can be analyzed as branches, beneficiaries, or peripheral movements of one or more of the regimes. The analysis of these three regimes will examine how their actions impact upon U.S. national interests, and how they interact with one another.

Iran

> "The most likely future challenge to the American position in the Middle East will come in the Persian Gulf from Iran. Iran ... will work diligently to squeeze the United States from the Gulf."[30]

Since the 1979 overthrow of America's ally, the Shah of Iran, the Islamic Republic of Iran has made opposition to the U.S. a cornerstone of its foreign policy. From the takeover of the U.S. embassy in Tehran, to the support of extremist movements in Lebanon engaged in acts of terror against the United States, Iran has continued a policy of antagonism toward America and American interests throughout the Middle East.

Currently, Iran is hampered in pursuing its national goals by severe economic problems. Analysts estimate the inflation rate is currently 40-50 percent and the unemployment rate is nearly 25 percent. This economic distress is squeezing Iran's ability to keep up its heavy purchases of state of the art conventional weapons, but is having little effect on Tehran's support for extremist groups.[31] To attempt to resolve this problem, Iran is reaching out to European and Japanese creditors to renegotiate payment of its eight billion dollar short term debt. The Europeans rationalize this assistance to President Rafsanjani as a way to strengthen his hand and champion a more pragmatic course in Iran. The U. S. position is that issues such as Iran's world wide support of extremist groups and opposition to the Arab-Israeli peace process must be addressed before normalizing economic relations.

Iran is mounting a two track national policy. On the one hand, pragmatic Iran has recently brokered the release of Western hostages in Lebanon, brokered a short cease fire between neighboring Armenia and Azerbaijan, and continued to court Western aid. On the other hand, revolutionary Iran has begun a massive arms buildup and provides safe havens for international terrorists, financial aid to extremist organizations, and Revolutionary Guards to train subversive and terrorist organizations in Lebanon and Sudan.[32]

The buildup of Iran's defense establishment is examined in terms of strategic buildup, conventional buildup, and unconventional preparation. The Tehran government spent half its budget on arms imports during the war with Iraq in the 1980s.[33] They are currently spending five to six billion dollars per year on defense, with two billion dollars of that dedicated to the procurement of new weapons from Russia, China, Eastern European countries, and North Korea.[34] In 1988, Rafsanjani stated "We must fully equip ourselves with defensive and offensive chemical, biological, and radiological weapons."[35]

The strategic buildup of Iran's military is being accomplished through the covert acquisition of nuclear technology and delivery systems. Russian intelligence sources claim that two of the three nuclear weapons found missing from the Semipalatinsk test range in Kazakhstan in 1991 have found their way to Iran. Other unsubstantiated sources claim that Iran may have two 40 kiloton (KT) warheads designed for Scud Mod C ballistic missiles, a 50 KT aerial bomb designed for delivery by MIG-27, and a 0.1 KT nuclear artillery shell; all reputedly smuggled from Kazakhstan.[36] The CIA cannot substantiate any possession of nuclear weapons by Iran.

Iranian attempts to procure nuclear technology was accelerated with the fall of the Soviet Union. As the borders of the former Communist state were opened, Iran recruited several Soviet nuclear scientists.[37] China is currently helping build a 27 kilowatt research reactor in Iran and has agreed to sell two more nuclear reactors to Iran.[38] Iran operates a clandestine network of ten nuclear research centers, has received bomb related technical help from Pakistan has signed a nuclear cooperation agreement with India, and receives additional nuclear assistance from Russia and North Korea. Estimates state that the next eight years is adequate for Iran to assemble a small nuclear device.[39]

The delivery systems procured or in the process of being procured include ballistic missiles, bombers, and fighter aircraft. North Korea is believed to have supplied 50 Scud Mod B missiles and 100 Scud Mod C missiles to Iran.[40] North Korea is also developing a Scud Mod D with a range of 1000 kilometers that is capable of delivering chemical and nuclear warheads. This missile is currently being developed exclusively for sale to Iran.[41]

Tehran has also bought 12 to 24 Backfire bombers. The Backfires can threaten all of the Gulf nations and can reach Israel in one hour flying at low altitude; less than one-half hour flying at high altitude.[42] The Iranians have also bought twenty five MIG-29s, and additional MIG-27s and MIG-31s.[43] In addition to delivering conventional weapons, some of these systems may in the future be configured for nuclear weapons.

The conventional buildup by the Iranians encompasses all aspects of the military from submarines to command and control aircraft to tanks. In addition to the systems previously mentioned, the Iranians have bought T-72 tanks, A-50 Mainstay aircraft (a Russian version of the AWACS) SU-24 fighter/bombers, three "K" class diesel submarines, and 10 MI-26 helicopters from Russia and China; and eight cruise missile from the Ukraine. In addition to these systems, Iran still retains the Iraqi aircraft flown into their country during Desert Shield/Desert Storm, to include two Adnan command and control aircraft.[44]

During late April and early May of 1992, Iran conducted a large amphibious landing exercise, designated Victory 3, on both sides of the Strait of Hormuz. The exercise covered 10,000 nautical square miles and exercised 45 destroyers, missile boats, logistics ships, and frigates; 150 speed boats; antisubmarine, minesweeping, and attack helicopters; air force fighter/bombers and electronic warfare aircraft; and special operations and Marine forces.[45] Victory 3 was clearly an offensive exercise designed to demonstrate Iranian capabilities to the Gulf countries. The exercise served as a warning of the ability of Iran to reach across the Gulf with ample force to establish a beachhead.

The Iranian clerics fear the regular armed forces of Iran because of their previous support of the Shah. The armed forces represent the only faction within Iran with the power to overthrow the current regime. As a result of this fear, the clerics retain control of the military and refuse to allow the professional military to conduct operations.[46]

The clerics have organized an independent military arm of the Islamic Republic, the Iranian Republic Guard Corps, or Pasdaran. This force actually was trained and organized, before the revolution, and served as the instrument that brought the revolution about.[47] The purpose of this force was to keep the military fragmented, make control by the religious leadership easier, provide a counterbalance to the military in the event of attempted coups, serve as a counter to leftist guerrillas, and serve as an instrument to export the Iranian revolution.[48] The role of the Pasdaran has been formalized in the Iranian constitution. The regular military is given the responsibility to preserve territorial integrity and political independence, while the Pasdaran is tasked to preserve the revolution.

The fragmentation of the Iranian defense structure is seen by many within the regime as a weakness. The Pasdaran have resisted the attempts of the regular army to merge into one unified defense force. In 1991, the army made an attempt to force the merger of all armed forces in the regime and did succeed in placing the air arm of the Pasdaran under the command of a regular Air Force general.[49]

The Iranian republic maintains regular forces of over 700,000; the Pasdaran's numbers are approximately 350,000. In addition, the People's Militia, trained and organized by the Pasdaran, numbers over three million.[50] As a result, the Pasdaran still maintain a significant force to ensure the loyalty of the regular military to the revolutionary regime.

The unconventional buildup of Iranian forces is accomplished through the training, aid, and funding of subversive and terrorist elements throughout the world. The most publicized subversive organization supported by Iran is the Hezbollah of Lebanon. Throughout the 1970s, Shia clergy received training at the religious centers in Iran. At these centers, they were indoctrinated with the radical teachings of the Ayatollah Khomeini.[51] The Lebanese Shia clergy then established the Hezbollah in 1982 with the assistance of over 1000 Pasdaran.[52] The Pasdaran established their headquarters in the town of Baalbek in the Bekaa valley and began training the Hezbollah for military operations against Israel, Lebanese government forces, and rival militias. The Pasdaran also aided the political movement of Hezbollah by building hospitals, clinics, and markets in the Baalbek region.[53] The Hezbollah, unlike most other extremist movements, is closely controlled and directed by Iran. Two of Iran's well known terror-diplomats supervised the formation of Hezbollah and the early bombing and kidnapping operations. Ali Akbar Mohtashemi, served as Iran's ambassador to Syria during the formative years of Hezbollah and directed the bombings and kidnappings in Beirut, as well as the TWA 847 hijacking.[54] Majid Kamal served as the Iranian Charge in Beirut during the early 1980s and was responsible for the training of the Hezbollah.[55]

The Iranian regime has also been responsible for providing training to various Palestinian extremist and terrorist organizations. The PLO of the late 70s/early 80's, the Popular Front for the Liberation of Palestine (PFLP), the PFLP-General Command (PFLP-GC), the Democratic Front for the Liberation of Palestine (DFLP), the Abu Nidal Organization (ANO), and the current Palestinian extremist groups, Hamas and Palestine Islamic Jihad.[56]

As will be examined in the later sections, Iran has provided training to various subversive elements operating throughout the Arabian Peninsula, Central Asia, and North Africa. The Iranian regime has also provided training to Afghanistan mujaheddin during the Soviet invasion and continues to assist the extremist elements in that country.[57]

The Iranians view terrorism as a valid tool to accomplish their political objectives, and acts of terrorism are approved at the highest level. In addition to foreign terrorist and extremist groups, the Iranians use their own citizens to conduct terrorist operations abroad. Throughout the second half of the 1980s and into the 1990s, Iranian assassins and kidnappers operated virtually uninhibited throughout Europe. Kidnapping and murder of opposition leaders in Turkey, Switzerland, France, and Italy have been documented.[58] The most public of these acts was the assassination of Shahpur Bakhtiar in a suburb of Paris on 6 August 1991. This act had been carefully planned for seven years and was carried out expertly by Iranian agents.[59]

Another aspect of Iranian terrorism is support for the international drug trade. Iran condones, if not directly supports, the flow of drugs across the porous borders of Iran, Pakistan, and Afghanistan.[60] During the first three years of the Soviet-Afghan war, opium production in Afghanistan nearly tripled due to the mujaheddin's need for funding.[61] Government estimates claim that roughly a third of the heroin produced in Afghanistan today reaches the United States. The major poppy growing regions in Afghanistan are controlled by the most radical political faction, Hezb-e-Islami, or the Islamic Party, led by Golbuddin Hekmatyar.[62]

A second notorious drug producing area that has increasingly come under the direction of Iran is the Bekaa valley of Lebanon. Three quarters of the Bekaa, or 5000 acres, is planted in hashish every year. In 1981, this crop yielded one billion dollars, In 1984, the valley produced 700 metric tons of hashish.[63]

Iran makes use of diplomatic cover to support the movements of its terrorists abroad. A bound and gagged Iranian opposition leader was found in the trunk of a car possessing diplomatic plates in Turkey in 1988. In 1990, an Iran Airways flight was held up in Switzerland for an hour and 15 minutes awaiting the arrival of two assassins, who eventually arrived in a car bearing Iranian diplomatic plates.[64] The Iranians use their embassies and diplomatic postings to provide cover for the direction of terrorism abroad. They provide diplomatic passports and the diplomatic pouch to transport heavily armed, highly trained terrorists.[65]

Iran's latest effort at exporting the Islamic revolution through terrorism is an alliance formed with the extremist Islamic regime in Sudan. The analysis of the background and threat of this expansion in Islamic extremism is addressed in later sections.

There are four national goals to which Iran is directing this effort: 1) regional dominance in the Persian Gulf, 2) an end to

Western influence in the Gulf, 3) export of the Islamic revolution, and 4) opposition to the Arab-Israeli peace process.[66] The purpose of the Iranian regime in the attempt to acquire nuclear weapons is to achieve the first goal of a regional hegemon in the Persian Gulf. The desire to be the dominating power in the Persian Gulf is based partly upon national and historical pride, but also on the factors of Iraqi power and oil pricing. After a draining eight year war with Iraq, in which Iraq demonstrated the ability to use chemical weapons, Iran become determined to attain military parity with Iraq. Prior to the 1991 Gulf War, Iraq appeared to be advancing rapidly toward the acquisition of nuclear weapons. To ensure the survival of the Islamic Republic, Iran launched its own nuclear program. Thus, one prime reason for attaining nuclear weapons is to maintain parity with Iraq. The second purpose behind the nuclear acquisition, as well as the conventional build up, is to threaten the GCC countries. Hampered by economic problems and determined to continue with a ten billion dollar rearming program, Iran strongly desires a rise in the price of oil. This is countered by the GCC countries who, with their large oil reserves, yield a strong influence in determining the price of oil. The Iranians hope to intimidate the GCC nations with their overwhelming military power and be the dominant influence in setting the price of oil.

The second national goal, to end Western influence in the Gulf, is primarily religious, but is also nationalistic as well.

As previously addressed, the Iranian regime desires regional hegemony. This is in direct conflict with U.S. strategic goals, which state a national interest in ensuring access to Persian Gulf oil. The only way to achieve the first goal of hegemony is to remove the U.S. from influence in the Gulf. The Iranian regime also views the U.S. as a corrupting influence on the traditional Islamic lifestyle. The goal is to remove the corrupting influence and strengthen the revolution, thus enabling its spread. The export of the revolution is being attempted through terrorism and support of subversive movements throughout the Middle East. These efforts are greatly aided by the assistance and cooperation with Sudan and factions in Afghanistan, which will be addressed in the following sections.

The opposition to the peace process is a response to Iran's perception of expansionist policies by Israel. Iran sees Israel as the unlawful occupier of the Moslem holy places in Jerusalem and the reincarnation of the Crusaders in occupying the land of dispossessed Moslems. Israel also acts as a Western influence in the region. Any peace agreement would be the result of a moderation in the politics of Arab states, a stance that Iran would find detrimental to their policy of the expansion of the Islamic revolution.

Sudan

When analyzing the country of Sudan, one might conclude that a nation so beset by troubles could not be a threat to a super power. As a result of those national problems, Sudan has emerged as a key country in the U.S. threat map. Sudan is beset by the majority of calamities that are found throughout the world today: civil war, starvation and famine, ethnic cleansing, bases for terrorist training, export of terrorism abroad, and an Islamic extremist government.

To gain an appreciation for the threat posed by Sudan, an examination of the background of its extremist leader is necessary. Hassan al-Turabi is the leader of the National Islamic Front (NIF). The NIF has slowly come to dominate the military regime that came to power on 30 June 1989. Turabi received his education in Oxford, England and Sorbonne, Paris. He returned to Sudan in 1964, assisted in the revolt against the military regime of General Abboud and became the secretary-general of the Moslem Brotherhood of Sudan.[67] In 1977, Turabi was named the Minister of Justice of Sudan and began to revise the laws of Sudan to bring them into conformity with the shari'a, the Islamic code of law. This posting, along with the assignment of another member of the Moslem Brotherhood to the Ministry of the Interior, enabled the Brotherhood to operate openly and aggressively after being underground during 1958-1964. In 1981, Turabi was appointed attorney-general of Sudan and succeeded in making the shari'a the law of the land in 1983. This decision rekindled the civil war, as it was highly unpopular with the Christians and animists in southern Sudan. The Sudan People's Liberation Army (SPLA) was formed and demanded a repeal of the shari'a for non-Moslems. Turabi was arrested in 1985 as a result of his part in implementing the shari'a. After a coup in 1985, which established another military regime, Turabi was released from prison, and founded the NIF, a coalition of Islamic parties dominated by the Moslem Brotherhood. During the 1989 coup, all leaders of political parties were arrested and placed in solitary confinement. Turabi was released after a couple of months and quickly assumed his place in the government of Lieutenant General Omar Hassen Ahmend al Bashir.[68]

The NIF is the only one of Sudan's thirty political parties allowed to participate in the current government of Sudan. Bashir realizes that his hold on the government is tenuous without the support of the strong Islamist movement. Likewise, Turabi knows that he must retain control of the military to effectively control the country.[69]

Turabi quickly consolidated his place in the government by forming an alliance with General Zubeir Salih, the number two man in the military regime, and bringing additional Islamists into the cabinet.[70] He has succeeded in purging more than 600 officers from the armed forces and ensured that all critical military commands are held by NIF members.[71]

In December 1990, Sudan declared itself an Islamic Republic and aligned itself with Libya and Iran. As a supporter of Iraq during Desert Shield/Desert Storm, Sudan found itself cut off from aid formerly supplied by the GCC and Egypt. In 1990, Sudan signed an alliance with Libya as an interim measure. This agreement was never the basis for a close alliance, as Qaddafi feared a Sudanese backed Islamist movement in Libya, and Turabi publicly stated that an Islamist government would soon arise in Libya.[72]

In December 1991, the alliance that Sudan had been seeking was formalized. President Rafsanjani of Iran led a 157 member delegation to Sudan. This delegation included the Foreign Minister, Minister of Defense, Minister of Intelligence, Commander of the Pasdaran, Minister of Commerce, and budget director.[73] The agreement resulting from this visit was for Iran to meet all of Sudan's oil needs, guarantee payments to China for Sudanese weapons and aircraft purchases (approximately 300 million dollars), and provide Revolutionary Guards to train Sudan's Popular Defense Forces. The Popular Defense Force is modelled after the Pasdaran and similarly serves Turabi as a counterweight to Sudan's military. The Pasdaran run the terrorist training camps that Sudan established as part of the agreement and provides troops to fight in Sudan's civil war.[74] Sudan is seen by Iran as the major success of the Islamic revolution, a nation that is established based upon the shari'a and the rule of the jurisconsult, the political guardianship of the community of believers by scholars trained in religious law.[75] Iran also sees Sudan as a base to penetrate Africa and the Arabian Peninsula. A reference to the map in Figure 5 reveals the central location of Sudan in the Middle East as

compared to the location of Iran to the eastern flank of the
targeted countries.

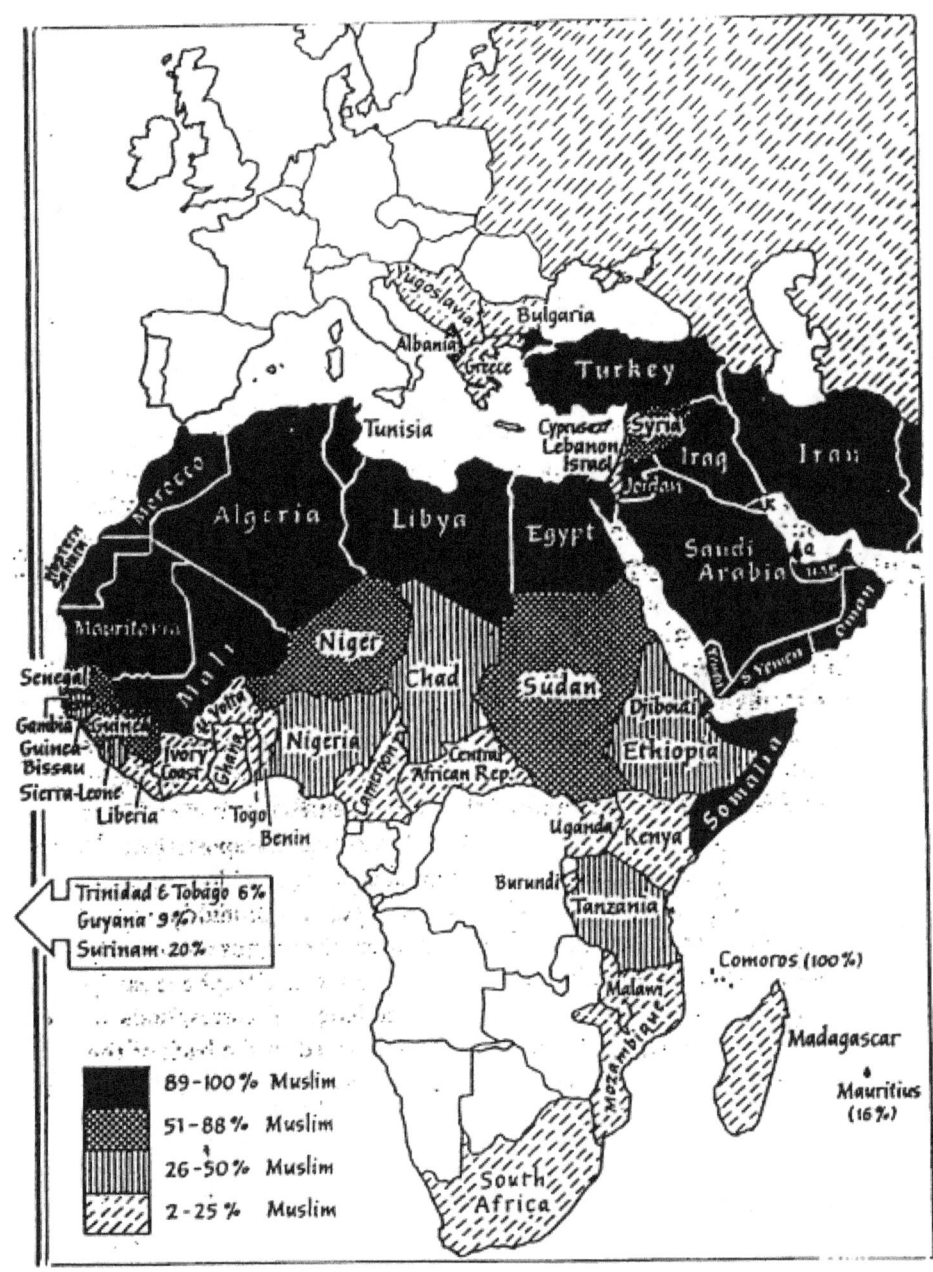

Figure 5. Geography of the Middle East and Africa - 1982. [78]

Sudan has become the focal point of terrorism in the Middle East. A list of just the Middle East terrorist and subversive organizations include the PFLP, DFLP, Hamas, Islamic Salvation Front (FIS) of Algeria, Tunisia's al-Nahda, Palestine Islamic Jihad, Yemen's al-Islah, Abu Nidal Organization, Egypt's Gama'a al-Islamiya and Al Jihad, and other smaller groups. In addition to these established groups, Sudan also provides training to individual terrorists from countries throughout the Middle East, and the horn of Africa.[76] Sudan provides the facilities for the Iranian Revolutionary Guard Corps (IRGC) to train these terrorist groups. The total number of IRGC currently in Sudan range from 2000 to 3000.[77] To direct the effort of the Revolutionary Guard, Iran has assigned Majid Kamal as ambassador to Sudan. Kamal engineered the 1979 U.S. embassy hostage taking in Tehran, supervised the creation of Lebanon's Hezbollah, and now oversees Iran's newest partner in terrorism.[79]

The Deputy Speaker of the Sudanese parliament recently defected to the United Kingdom and revealed that Sudan has clearly adopted many of Iran's methods of terrorism. The terrorist training is under the direct control of Turabi. All Sudanese diplomats are sent to Iran for training prior to posting throughout the world. General guidance in training the terrorists comes from Tehran.[80]

Countries throughout the Middle East have accused Sudan of providing passports and false documentation to extremists entering their countries.[81]The recent terrorist acts in New York

City reveal a heavy use of Sudanese diplomatic cover. The spiritual leader of the accused terrorists, Sheikh Omar Abdel Rahman, was able to get a visa through the U.S. embassy in Sudan in May of 1990 to enter the U.S., even though he was on the State Department's list of suspected terrorists.[82] Five of the eight suspects arrested for planning to blow up the United Nations building, the FBI building, and the Lincoln and Holland Tunnels possessed Sudanese passports.[83] The apparent leader, Siddig Ibrahim Siddig Ali, told a government informant that he had access to diplomatic plates for gaining access to the U.N. building.[84] Two Sudanese diplomats, both suspected intelligence officers, have also been implicated in the bombing plot.[85]

The internal problems in Sudan stem from the causes of the civil war. Since independence in 1956, the northern Moslem Arabs have attempted to dominate the southern Christian and animist Africans. The religious and ethnic conflict has raged for almost forty years. The current source of conflict is the refusal of the NIF dominated government to repeal the shari'a for the non-Moslem south.[86] The civil war is placing an immense drain on an already impoverished country. Estimates are that the civil war is costing the government one million dollars per day. This drain on the economy has driven Sudan to make agreements with pariah nations to receive funding and arms to fight the civil war.[87]

Complicating the civil war is the famine in the horn of Africa. Western agencies have attempted to provide humanitarian relief to the southern Sudanese, but have been expelled or harassed, for fear that the humanitarian aid is supporting the rebellion.[88] The Sudanese have also sold donated grain to buy arms to fight the people that the grain was intended to feed.[89] The decade of civil war has left 800,000 dead, five million refugees, and 700,000 in imminent danger of starvation; this is from a total population of 25 million.[90]

In addition to the civil war against the SPLA and the famine in southern Sudan, the Sudanese government has engaged in several periods of ethnic cleansing. Sudan contains twenty different ethnic groups, nine of which are predominantly Moslem and eleven of which are predominantly non-Moslem. In November 1991 and early 1992, the Sudanese government uprooted 400,000 non-Arabs from the outskirts of Khartoum and transported them fifty kilometers into the desert with no shelter, food, or water.[91] In March 1992, as the Sudanese army launched an offensive against the SPLA, one of the objectives was to eradicate the Nuba, a dark skinned people of mixed religious beliefs who lived in the border areas near the rebel held territory.[92]

The primary goal of the Sudan government is to end the civil war. The agreement with Iran provides arms, fuel, and advisors to proceed toward this goal. However, the ability of the government to defeat the rebels is complicated by the vastness of the country and limited by a two month dry season during which it can conduct offensives.[93] Until the Sudanese government moderates its stand with the shari'a and ethnic cleansing, the rebellion in the south will continue.

Turabi has stated that he foresees one Islamic community in the horn of Africa consisting of Sudan, Somalia, Ethiopia, Eritrea, and Djibouti.[94] As will be seen in the section on East Africa, Turabi may be taking a proactive role in this formation by training extremists from Ethiopia and Eritrea, and supplying arms to factions in Somalia. As a leading member of the Moslem Brotherhood, Turabi prescribes to the General Principles of the organization, among them, "the return to the foundation of Islam brings together the sects of Islam" and "The Arab nation is one nation".[95] These principles allow the Sudanese Sunnis to cooperate with the Iranian Shi'ites and provide the vehicle for the overriding goal of Turabi: The unification of the Arab world under one Islamic nation.

Sudan threatens the national interests of the U.S. by their attempts to subvert the nations that geographically control vital strategic chokepoints. Their aid to factions in Egypt threaten our access to the Suez Canal and endangers a government that has been a steadfast ally of the U.S. for fifteen years. Their support for subversive elements in Yemen, Somalia, and Eritrea threaten our access through the Red Sea via the chokepoint of the Bab el Mandeb. Finally, their sponsorship of terrorism is a threat to Americans and American interests throughout the world as was demonstrated by their insidious involvement in the World Trade Center bombing and the related plots.

Afghanistan

The term jihad, or holy war, is often used by Islamic groups as a rallying cry to incite volunteers to fight the infidels or other perceived enemies. These requests are most often unanswered or of short duration. The one exception to this in our recent history was the response of the Islamic world to the invasion of Afghanistan by the Soviet Union. The cry for holy war was answered by Moslems from around the world, predominantly from the Middle East. This flow of volunteers to join the mujaheddin was encouraged by the West and the moderate Arab regimes. The mujaheddin were heavily funded by individual contributions as well as aid from governments. The factions that fought the war developed identities and were classified as pro-Western, anti-Communist, nationalist, or Islamic extremist. The labels that were applied to the factions did not affect the flow of funds and arms to them from the West. The U.S. tended to favor the strongest and best organized movements, allowing the Inter-Services Intelligence (151) of Pakistan to distribute arms to the factions.

The faction that has grown to threaten the interests of the United States is the Hezb-e-Islamic, or the Islamic Party, led by Golbuddin Hekmatyar. The Islamic Party has from the beginning claimed to be an extremist, anti-Western Islamic movement. Regardless of their claims, the CIA provided 25-50 percent of the weapons supplied to the mujaheddin to the Islamic Party.[96] The estimates of the cost of arms supplied to Hekmatyar alone is more than one billion dollars. Hekmatyar's faction currently controls much of eastern Afghanistan and is engaged in a civil war against his rival faction leader, Burhaddin Rabbani, leader of the Islamic League. Hekmatyar has besieged the capital of Kabul for 22 months with artillery and rockets. His seige has killed more than 10,000 Afghan citizens.[97]

In addition to fighting the civil war, Hekmatyar is continuing to train volunteers from throughout the world in his twenty training camps in eastern Afghanistan. The volunteers who once were trained to fight the Soviets in Afghanistan are now being returned to their native countries to continue the jihad. The veterans have taken their war abroad to Algeria, Azerbaijan, Bangladesh, Bosnia, Burma, China, Egypt, India, Morocco, Pakistan, Sudan, Tadzhikistan, Tunisia, Uzbekistan, Yemen, and the United States.[98]

Conservative estimates report 3000-4000 foreign volunteers were in Afghanistan at any one time, with possibly as many as 40,000 foreigners having fought there during the entire period of the war. Currently; the number of foreigners training and fighting in Afghanistan are estimated at less than 1000. The civil war is not the drawing card that the war against the Soviet Union was.[99] Some estimates state that Hekmatyar's Islamic Party may have contained a cumulative 16,000-20,000 foreign volunteers.[100] In the five years since the Soviets withdrew, radicals from forty nations have come to Afghanistan for training.[101]

Hekmatyar has strong bonds with two extremist leaders in the Arab world who made many visits to the Peshawar, Pakistan camps of Hekmatyar. Hekmatyar struck up a personal and ideological friendship with Sheikh Abdel Rahman of Egypt during his visits in 1988 and 1990. In July of 1993, Hekmatyar offered Rahman political asylum in Afghanistan.[102] Hassan al-Turabi of Sudan has been a visitor and supporter of Hekmatyar since the years of the Soviet occupation. Turabi has recently been meeting with Hekmatyar and Rabbani to attempt to mediate an agreement between the warring factions and most likely to conduct a "board meeting" on their training and transshipment of terrorists and subversives.[103]

The CIA has recently initiated an attempt to buy back unused surface-to-air Stinger missiles which were supplied to the mujaheddin. Congress has authorized more than $65 million for the buy back of the missiles over the last three years. The concern is that the missiles could fall into the hands of terrorist or hostile regimes that may use them against civilian or military aircraft.[104] Already missiles supplied to the mujaheddin have turned up in Iran, Qatar, and North Korea.[105] U.S. analysts estimate that as many as 400 unfired missiles may now be under the control of various Afghan commanders. Hekmatyar commented, while on a visit to Tehran last fall, "The Afghan government does not intend to allow even a round of ammunition to be taken out of Afghanistan."[106] Another comment that came out of the taped transcripts from the World Trade Center bombing trials leaves one wondering to where Hekmatyar may have dispatched Stingers. Siddig Ibrahim Siddig Ali, the Sudanese suspected of being the major figure in the New York bombing conspiracy was recorded with the following quote: ". . .we'll hit them with missiles and we will take hostages."[107]

The goal of Golbuddin Hekmatyar is to establish an Islamic Republic in Afghanistan that would resemble the ones in Iran and Sudan. He stockpiled weapons from the CIA to make war for years to come. He controls the huge heroin drug trade coming out of Afghanistan to fund his army.[108] He runs training camps for his ideological allies, Iran and Sudan, in return for their assistance in the sale and trafficking of drugs.

The Islamic Party began at Kabul University as an outgrowth of the Moslem Brotherhood and continues to pursue a course strictly guided by the Moslem Brotherhood of Egypt.[109] Hence the ideological affinity of Hekmatyar with Rahman and al-Turabi. Following the principles of the Moslem Brotherhood, Hekmatyar will strive to establish the Islamic state, support the spread of the Islamic revolution, and remain anti-Western. It appears only a matter of time until Hekmatyar heads an Islamic Republic of Afghanistan and consolidates his position as the third leg of the triad of Islamic terror.

The radical factions in Afghanistan threaten U.S. national interests through their training of subversives that threaten to overthrow pro-Western Arab regimes. Their support for terrorism and drug trafficking also represent dangers to U.S. interests.

III. The Threatened Areas

The Persian Gulf

All three of the U.S. national interests are at stake in the Persian Gulf: access to oil, access to strategic waterways, and support for U.S. allies in the region. The Iranians have attempted through subversion and overt military action to intimidate and dominate the Gulf countries.

The divisions among the populations of the Gulf nations provide an environment for subversion by the Iranian Shi'ites. A brief analysis is provided of each nation that faces a threat from the Iranians. Shias compose between 5 and 10 percent of the Saudi population. They constitute between 40 and 60 percent of the work force in the vital oil industry. 1n1979 and 1980, Iranian inspired demonstrations took place in the Eastern Province of Saudi Arabia. The Saudis reacted by redressing the economic disadvantages of the Shia community. This remedy worked in the short term and appealed to the Shia middle class. The Shia lower class will continue to be vulnerable to Iranian propaganda if they see no improvement in living conditions.[110]

Iran continues to challenge the sovereign independence of Bahrain. Bahrain is ruled by a Sunni monarch, but 72 percent of Bahraini citizens are Shia. In 1981, a group of Iranian backed plotters attempted a coup in Bahrain to establish an Islamic form of government similar to Iran. The plot was foiled, but the attempt served as a warning to the fragile nature of peace in the region. Bahrain, like Saudi Arabia, has concentrated on improving the human conditions of its Shia citizens.[111]

In 1983, Kuwait became the next object of Iranian attempts at instability. Kuwait's population is 25 percent Shia and that segment of the population has close relations with the Iranian Shias. The wave of bombings that occurred in 1983 were part of a grand plot to assault the American embassy and seven other targets. The Islamic Jihad, considered a cover name for the Hezbollah, took credit for the bombings.[112]

The United Arab Emirates (UAE) were the next country of the GCC to be directly confronted by Iran, as the Iranians expelled expatriate workers from the UAE side of the oil producing island of Abu Musa. The Iranians have recently begun construction of military facilities on the island. Iran had previously exerted a claim to the two Tunb islands as well.[113]

These examples indicate that Iran has continued to attempt to impose its ideology upon the GCC countries since 1979. As Iran modernizes its forces, we can expect the continuation of threats to the Gulf states and the threat to the West of blocking the Strait of Hormuz.

North Africa

The primary U.S. national security interests that are at stake in North Africa are access to strategic waterways and support of U.S. allies. The area is flanked by two very important chokepoints: the Strait of Gibraltar and the Suez Canal. Key allies in North Africa include the reliable nations of Morocco and Egypt, which coincidentally control the chokepoints. In addition to the countries of North Africa, we must be concerned with the effect of disruption in North Africa to our allies in Europe.

The five nations of North Africa are all confronted with Islamic extremist movements.[114] Due to the strength of the current regimes, Morocco, Tunisia, and Libya face a limited threat from the Islamists, but could have a greater threat to deal with if social and economic conditions worsen in those countries. Algeria and Egypt face Islamic extremist movements that are a serious threat to overturn the current regimes.

The Islamic extremist movement in Egypt began in 1970 when the Gama'a-el-Islamiya, or Islamic Group, emerged as a successor to the outlawed Moslem Brotherhood. Other extremist groups were formed shortly afterward, the most notable of which was Al Jihad. The two groups have evolved separately, but maintain joint committees for operations, propaganda, and finance.[115]

Al Jihad rose to prominence in Egypt on 6 October 1981, when the leader of the country, Anwar Sadat, was assassinated by an army officer, Lieutenant Khaled Islambouli, who was a member of an army cell of Al Jihad. This cell was led by Colonel Aboud el-Zomar, a military intelligence officer; the group's spiritual mentor was Sheikh Omar Abdel Rahman. An uprising was launched in the aftermath of Sadat's assassination, timed to take advantage of disorder in the government. This uprising left more than a hundred Egyptian policemen dead before it was quelled. The uprising was led by the Gama'a which also looked to Omar Abdel Rahman for spiritual guidance.[116]

The extremists turned much of their attention abroad after the uprising failed to topple the Egyptian government. The call for jihad in Afghanistan appealed to the Egyptian extremists, and many members of Gama'a and Al Jihad travelled to Peshawar, Pakistan to join the mujaheddin. The extremists claim that 20,000 Egyptians fought for the mujaheddin during the war. The Egyptian government states the number is only 2500, and at least 200 of those have returned to oppose the government.[117] The Pakistan government has records of 6170 foreigners who have entered that country in route to join the mujaheddin, but also conclude that many more volunteers were never registered by the Pakistani government.[118]

The network for the movement of smuggling people and arms from Egypt to Afghanistan was established in 1983 by Mohammed Shawki Islambouli, the brother of Sadat's assassin.[119] The pipeline for recruiting volunteers for the mujaheddin is through two groups considered to be moderate fundamentalists: the Moslem Brotherhood and the World Muslim League. During the war Omar Abdel Rahman made visits to the camps in Peshawar in 1988 and 1990. During these visits, he was hosted by his Gama'a follower, Islambouli and kindled a friendship with Golbuddin Hekmatyar. The Afghan war became one of Abdel Rahman's passions to such an extent that two of his sons fought there and his extremist followers directed their attention to the war and away from Abdel Rahman's other passion, the installation of an Islamist regime in Egypt.[120] As the Afghan struggle against the Soviet Union ended, the Arab volunteers returned home along the same underground that Islambouli had established in 1983.

By July of 1989, the Egyptian extremists were utilizing training camps and safe havens run by Hassan al-Turabi in Sudan. Turabi and Abdel Rahman became acquainted during the late 1970's, and as fellow members of the Moslem Brotherhood shared the vision of one Arab nation built on Islamic principles. The two extremist leaders also shared a passion for the Afghan war, Turabi being a frequent visitor of the mujaheddin camps as well.[121]

In the spring of 1992, a wave of violence erupted in Egypt as the Gama'a, led by veterans of the Afghanistan war, began their campaign to overthrow the government and establish an Islamic republic.[122] Sheikh Abdel Rahman sanctioned fund raising raids on stores and shops owned by Coptic Christians.[123] Rahman continued to preach his virulent brand of Islam, distorting the Koran to suit his narrow, violent agenda, and thus justifying assassination, bombings, and indiscriminate acts of terror against innocent lystanders.[124]

The tactics of Gama'a and Al Jihad are reputed to be of opposite scope. Gama'a attacks "from below", conducting minor acts of terrorism such as shooting foreign tourists, setting off bombs in public squares, and shooting government ministers and low ranking police. Al Jihad concentrates on attacking "from above", shooting high level political figures and building secret networks in the army, police and other state institutions.[125]

The extremist campaign is having the effect of worsening economic and social conditions in Egypt by targeting the income producing tourist trade. The violence directed against tourists is depriving the government of much needed currency. The violence has taken a toll on the Egyptian populace with over 320 deaths and 700 wounded since the campaign began in 1992.[126] The Gama'a is suspected to have several thousand active members and as many as 200,000 supporters. The major extremist groups are suspected to operate out of bases in Sudan and have training camps in Afghanistan.[127] Iran is suspected to actively fund the movements and enough evidence has been found to lead Thomas McNamera, the U.S. State Department's counterterrorism officer, to conclude that "Iran is the major underwriter of terrorism in Egypt".[128]

Declining oil revenues, crushing unemployment, rampant inflation, and widespread corruption in Algeria in the 1980s led to the creation of the Islamic Salvation Front (FIS) in March, 1989.[129] The organization has its base of support among the illiterate and poor who suffer the most from economic unrest. The FIS quickly gained influence by providing social services and promising answers to the pressing economic problems. In the 26 December 1991 parliamentary elections, the FIS won 188 of the 206 seats. By comparison, the ruling National Liberation Front was only able to win fifteen seats. A runoff for the remaining 224 seats was set for 16 January 1992, with the FIS poised to win a parliamentary majority.[130] Before the elections could be held, the Algerian army conducted a coup d'etat to prevent the FIS from forming a government. The motivation for the coup was to prevent an Islamist regime along the lines of Iran and Sudan from taking power.[131]

The FIS has launched a campaign to take by force what was denied by the ballot. The campaign of terror has resulted in the death of 3500 Algerians; the assassination of Mohammed Boudiaf, the military's appointed president; and the death of 300 members of the security force and other government off icials.[132]

As unemployment and inflation continue to rise, many elements within the army are sympathizing with the FIS. The potential for a deadly civil war is very high. It is estimated that an Algerian civil war would unleash 500,000 refugees on France and provide a destabilizing effect on Tunisia and Morocco. [133]

The question arises as to who provides the training and funding for the FIS. The familiar refrain is repeated again. Camps in Sudan run by the Iranian Pasdaran provide training to the Algerian extremists. Their leadership is provided by the "Afghans", or the Algerian volunteers who fought in Afghanistan.[134] The motive for the involvement of Iran is the export of the Islamic revolution; Sudan's motivation is the eventual establishment of one Islamic Arab nation.

The disintegration of Algeria would affect U.S. national interests by destabilizing allies in the region and potentially endangering shipping in the Mediterranean Sea. The refugee flow to France would create economic and security problems for a key U.S. ally. An Islamist regime in Algeria would likely support subversive elements in neighboring Tunisia and Morocco and lead to the destabilization of these U.S. allies. An extremist regime in Algeria would also gain control of modern weaponry with which to threaten U.S. forces and commercial interests in the Mediterranean.

Israel, Lebanon, and Jordan

Israel, Lebanon, and Jordan are all threatened by extremist movements within their borders, as well as the spillover from the neighboring countries. The primary threats are the Hamas in Israel, the Hezbollah in Lebanon, and the Vanguard of the Islamic Youth in Jordan.

Hamas was created prior to the intifada in the occupied territories. It evolved from the Moslem Brotherhood of Palestine and, as with most other breakaway movements from the Brotherhood, differs from that organization by their preferred use of violence and terrorism as a means to attain their goals. Israel actually nurtured the growth of the Islamic fundamentalist movement in Palestine as a counterbalance to the more secular PLO.[135]

The goal of Hamas is to establish an Islamic republic, not only in the occupied territories, but throughout Palestine. They see an Islamic Palestine as a pre-cursor to a greater pan-Arab Islamic union.[136] Hamas has eroded the support for the PLO in the occupied areas. The PLO's support for Iraq in the Gulf War lost the organization the backing of the GCC nations. This loss of support and the gains made by Hamas were key ingredients that led the PLO to the peace table with Israel. The PLO sees peace with Israel as a way to retain power and gain financial support.[137]

Hamas is in a strong position to challenge the PLO should elections be held in an independent Palestinian state. The movement claims support from a majority of Palestinians in Gaza and at least 30-40 percent of West Bank Arabs.[138] In recent internal elections on the West Bank, Hamas defeated the PLO.[139] Sudan provides sanctuary and training bases for Hamas and Iran provides funding and a headquarters in Tehran.[140]

Hezbollah was created in 1982 by the Iranian Pasdaran and Lebanese Shia clergy trained at religious centers in Iran. The foot soldiers of Hezbollah were recruited from young urban poor around Beirut arid their rural counterparts in the south of Lebanon and the Bekaa Valley. The goal of Hezbollah is to establish an Islamic state in Lebanon similar to the regime in Iran.[141]

The terror campaign waged against the West in Lebanon during the 1980s succeeded in the removal of much of the Western influence and consolidated Hezbollah's position in the country. Hezbollah was legally recognized as a political party in Lebanon in 1992 and won eight of the 128 seats in parliamentary elections.[142]

Hezbollah continues to maintain strong militia forces in south Lebanon and launched 330 attacks against civilian and military targets in Israel in 1993.[143] Recent attempts have been made to conduct joint operations with Hamas. Hezbollah claims that it desires to put the resistance against Israel into the hands of Hamas and proposes coordinating, planning, and carrying out combined security operations.[144]

The Iranians continue to fund Hezbollah and provide control and guidance to the movement. Sudan provides sanctuary and training camps for the movement and may have provided logistical support for their 1992 bombing of the Israeli embassy in Buenos Aires.[145]

The Islamist threat to Jordan comes from subversive and political movements. The Islamists won thirty two of eighty seats in the lower house of parliament in the 1989 elections. They also gained five cabinet positions and the speakership of the lower house.[146] This was later moderated in the 1993 elections, where the Islamists only retained eighteen seats.[147] Nonetheless, the political strength of the Islamists is significant, and given the failing health of King Hussein, combined with a teetering economy, the Islamists could be poised for an attempt to gain power in Jordan.

The Iranians provide support to the Vanguard of the Islamic Youth via the PFLP-GC.[148] The Jordanians closely monitor the movement, but could have difficulty coping with them should they gain strength and cooperate more closely with other extremists movements in the area.

The threat to the U.S. in this area is clearly the survival of Israel. The extremist movements desire to eradicate the state and replace it with an Islamic regime that would be anti-Western in philosophy. As long as Israel remains a dependable ally in this important part of the world, they will continue to merit our support.

Central Asia

Prior to the fall of the Soviet Union, Iran and the Islamic Party of Afghanistan were supporting Islamic extremist movements in the Central Asian republics of the USSR. This support and interest continues as the newly independent republics strive to establish their national identity. The spiritual appeal of the Islamic revolution, the cultural history of the Persians, and an outlet to the sea are the factors that Iran hopes will give it a dominant position with the republics.[149] However, the Central Asian republics are more closely linked to Turkey ethnically (the majority are Turkomans) and religiously (the majority are Sunni). The new governments of these republics are oriented toward a secular form of government and a capitalist form of economy to take advantage of their rich resources.[150]

The Iranians, Sudanese, and Afghans have all been involved with training subversive elements within Central Asia, particularly in Tajikistan. The Iranians have been financing the Islamic Renaissance Party of Tajikistan and providing arms and training via Golbuddin Hekmatyar in Afghanistan.[151] The Sudanese have been involved by providing training at Iran's Shandi base near Obdurman, Sudan. The groups of Tajiks that have trained there received instruction on tactics, use of infantry weapons and artillery, and intelligence gathering.[152]

The primary importance of this area to the West is that the nuclear weapons of Kazakhstan do not fall into the hands of the extremists. Kazakhstan has agreed to transfer the weapons to Russia, but this is not an instant process. Kazakhstan possesses enough nuclear warheads to make it fifteen times the nuclear power of Great Britain.[153] Of slightly less importance is the oil reserves and mineral wealth of this area. Access to these materials could prove vital to the West should access to Persian Gulf oil be endangered.

East Africa and Yemen

Islamic extremist movements are beginning a gradual growth along the coast of East Africa. This area is fertile ground for the movements due to widespread poverty, corruption, and disorder. Sudan is active in supporting extremist activity in the horn of Africa in fulfillment of the previously mentioned goal of one Islamic community in the region.

Sudan has been the conduit of arms, supplied by Iran, to several Islamic factions and clan leaders in Somalia, including

Mohammed Farah Aidid.[154] Eritrea recently intercepted a group of the Eritrean Islamic Jihad (EIJ) crossing the border from Sudan and killed 21 members of the unit. Among the dead were Afghans, Pakistanis, and Moroccans - strong indications that the EIJ is not an internal Eritrean movement.[155]

Aldu Aju, the deputy speaker of the Sudanese parliament who defected to Great Britain in early 1994, claimed his government was supporting extremists in Ethiopia.[156] The Ethiopian extremist group Ogaden Islamic Union is reported to be supported by military advisors from Afghanistan, Sudan, and Iran.[157]

Across the Red Sea, the fragile unification of the Yemen Arab Republic and the People's Democratic Republic of Yemen threatens to break apart into civil war. The political strife is complicated by unemployment of 40 percent and inflation of 300 percent. The Islamist party, Islah, holds 62 of the 301 seats in parliament and the leader of Islah, Sheikh al-Ahmar, is the speaker. He is also third in line of succession to head the government. The military wing of Islah wages a terror campaign against the two parties that represented the governments of the two former republics. Yemen has maintained training camps for Middle East terrorist groups for at least twenty years. The country has become a stopover point for "Afghans" returning to Africa from Afghanistan. The hidden hand of Iran and Sudan may be at play to gain control of the strategic Bab el Mandeb chokepoint by establishing Islamist regimes in Yemen, Somalia, and Eritrea.[158]

An Islamist movement, the Islamic Party of Kenya, is also blooming in Kenya where the two million Moslems make up eight percent of the population. Tanzania and Mozambique have also experienced unrest from their Moslem populations. In South Africa, Ibrahim Rausool, leader of the "Call of Islam", was elected to the African National Congress executive in the West Cape, giving Moslems a voice in the South African government and visibility in a strife torn, strategically located nation.[159]

The interests endangered from Islamic extremism in this section of the world is the access to critical waterways and vital minerals. As previously stated, 15 percent of the world's commerce passes through the waters of the Middle East. Any threat to restricting traffic through the Bab el Mandeb would be of interest to the United States. Forty percent of petroleum flowing to the West passes via the southern Cape route. A hostile regime in South Africa could threaten the West's energy lifeline. South Africa's deposits of chromium, platinum, and manganese are essential to the U.S. production of automobiles, tanks, and high performance aircraft. South Africa contains 82 percent of the world's chromium reserves, 75 percent of manganese reserves, and 90 percent of platinum reserves. The U.S. cannot reach surge capacities during mobilization without continued access to sizeable quantities of these minerals. U.S. domestic deposits could not make up for a shortfall should access to these materials be lost.[160]

United States

    On 26 February 1993, the illusion of America being safely distant from the extremist threat of the Middle East was shattered when the World Trade Center was bombed. The investigation launched to discover the perpetrators of the bombing uncovered a well financed, well trained, and tightly organized group of Islamic extremists operating in the New York City area. The suspects included a group of individuals from various Middle East countries, a U.S. citizen, and a Puerto Rican. The occupations of the suspects ranged from a well educated chemical engineer to a pizza deliveryman to an unemployed immigrant.[161] The common thread among the suspects was their attendance at the Al Salam mosque in Jersey City and the spiritual mentorship of Omar Abdel Rahman, who preaches at the mosque.[162]

    Another common thread that is seen in the organization that conducted the bombing is their involvement with the war in Afghanistan. In July 1990, Omar Abdel Rahman arrived in the United States. His sponsor upon his arrival was Mustafa Shalabi, an Egyptian who ran the Moslem Brotherhood sponsored Alkifah Refugee Center in Brooklyn. The purpose of the Center was to recruit and train young men from the surrounding Moslem community for the war in Afghanistan.[163] One of the men convicted in the World Trade Center bombing, Egyptian born Mahmud Abouhalima, was an experienced commander from the war in Afghanistan. Two suspects currently pending trial for related bombing plots were also Afghanistan veterans. Siddig Ibrahim Siddig Ali, a Sudanese native, was a troop commander and Clement Rodney Hampton-El, a black American hospital technician, served as a medic in the war.[164] Ramzi Ahmed Yousef, an Iraqi veteran of Afghanistan, travelled from Pakistan to the U. S. with Ahmad Ajaj, a Palestinian fresh from Afghanistan, who was found in the possession of bomb making manuals. Ajaj was found guilty in the World Trade Center bombing; Yousef remains at large.[165] In addition to the foot soldiers who were involved in the bombings, Omar Abdel Rahman himself was a visitor to Afghanistan in 1988 and 1990.

A chronology of actual and planned terrorist activity in the New York City area reveals a series of well financed, carefully planned acts. In November 1990, the Jewish extremist, Rabbi Meir Kahane, was murdered in New York City. At the time of the incident and during the subsequent trial, the murder appeared to be an isolated act of violence. During the World Trade Center investigation, the Kahane murder was linked to the followers of Abdel Rahman. El Sayyid Nosair was convicted of weapons charges in relation to the Kahane murder. While in jail, Nosair was visited by his fellow members of the Al Salam mosque, who would later be indicted for terrorist acts of their own.[166]

In 1992, Mustafa Shalabi, the organizer of the Alkifah Refugee Center, was found murdered in his Brooklyn apartment. This act occurred after a disagreement between Shalabi and Abdel Rahman as to the direction the Center should take. Abdel Rahman insisted on using the Center to support the Islamist movement in Egypt. The murder of Shalabi remains unsolved, but Abdel Rahman is suspected of sanctioning the murder, and Mahmud Abouhalima, his driver and bodyguard, is the prime suspect.[167]

February 1993 marked the occurrence of the bombing of the World Trade Center. During the investigation, the services of an informer within the terrorist network were engaged by the Federal Bureau of Investigation (FBI) to gain access to the ring. The informer enabled the FBI to conduct a raid in early July 1993 to arrest eight extremists in the act of making bombs. The bombings, timed to occur prior to the July 4th holiday, were targeted at the UN building, the FBI building in New York City, the Lincoln tunnel, and the Holland tunnel.[168]

The taped recordings conducted by the informant revealed additional plans to assassinate UN Secretary-General Boutros Boutros-Ghali, U.S. Senator Alfonse D'Amato, and New York Assemblyman Dov Hikind.[169] Investigators uncovered plans that resulted in eleven additional members of the extremist organization being charged with conspiracy to assassinate Egyptian President Hosni Mubarak during a visit to the U.S. The first attempt at the visiting President's life in April was foiled, as Mubarak cancelled a trip to New York City. Plans were made to attempt the act again in September 1993, when Mubarak was scheduled to attend the opening of the UN General Assembly. Among those charged were Siddig Ali, the Sudanese ringleader of the July 1993 bombing plot, and Hampton-El, the American Moslem charged in the July bombing plot.[170]

Tape recordings between the informers and Siddig Ali revealed a plot to kidnap influential Americans and ransom them for the release of their fellow Moslems held in connection with the World Trade Center bombing. Siddig Ali claimed the idea originated with Nosair, who was in jail for Kahane's murder. The two Americans whom the plotters considered kidnapping were Richard Nixon and Henry Kissinger.[171]

Several troubling observations are made of the events centered on the World Trade Center bombings. First, the matter of funding. U.S. intelligence officers have strong evidence that Iran provides funds to Omar Abdel Rahman.[172] During a confession made under torture in Egypt, Abouhalima stated the group received funds from Iran, the Egyptian group Gama'a, and the German offices of the Moslem Brotherhood.[173] Funds were readily available, as Mohammed Salameh, a poor, unemployed illegal immigrant charged in the World Trade Center bombing, was able to offer five million dollars for bail.[174]

A second observation is the charges that Siddig Ali and Hampton-El were suspected of trafficking in opium. Both men are veterans of the Afghanistan war and supposedly are one of the American connections for the lucrative export of opium from Afghanistan.[175]

The third observation is the use of diplomatic privileges by the plotters. Ahmad Ajaj, who was convicted in-the World Trade

Center bombing held four passports: a Jordanian passport under his name and British, Swedish, and Saudi passports under assumed names.[176] Siddig Ali planned to acquire diplomatic license plates to allow a bomb laden van access to the UN building.[177] Two Sudanese diplomats serving at the UN were implicated in the bombing plot: Siraj Yousif, the counsellor to the Sudanese mission and Ahmed Mohammed, the third secretary. Both are suspected Sudanese intelligence officers.[178]

The stated purpose of the terrorist campaign was to "express anger with the U.S. support of Israel" and to "punish the U.S. for its support of Israel and secular Arab governments like Egypt".[179] The suspected hidden involvement of Iran and Sudan and the link with Afghanistan leave the suspicion of a connection with the planned wave of terror in the U.S. and current extremist activities in the Middle East. A weakening of U.S. support for Israel, Egypt, and the GCC nations as a result of domestic terrorist acts would serve the goals of the Islamists.

The probable motive for Islamist terrorism in the U.S. is to create a theatrical display of the susceptibility of U.S. citizens to acts of terror if the U.S. continues support for Israel, Egypt, and other moderate Arab regimes. The campaign of terrorism(s) employed by the Islamists include the theatrical acts in the U.S. targetted at public opinion, as well as the acts in the Middle East directed at overthrowing the moderate regimes. This strategy of blending different targets of terrorism to achieve a specific goal is alarming.

IV. THE NETWORK

Islamic extremists are aided, financed, and provided safe havens in their movements by the governments of Iran and Sudan, and by the various factions in Afghanistan, particularly the Islamic Party of Golbuddin Hekmatyar. There is another network that sympathizes with and provides assistance to Islamic extremist groups. This network is the Moslem Brotherhood. Although the Brotherhood today is primarily concerned with social services, political participation, and campaigning against corruption, drugs, prostitution, and other social ills, there are strong elements within the organization that take the extremist view of violence and revolution as a means to achieve their goal of one Islamic nation based upon Islamic law and legislation.

During most of its history, the Moslem Brotherhood actively used violence as a method to achieve its goals. Every Egyptian leader from 1948 until the death of Anwar Sadat has either been assassinated or the object of an assassination attempt by the Moslem Brotherhood of. Egypt.[180] As late as 1982, the Moslem Brotherhood of Syria prepared for an all out assault to overthrow the ruling Ba'ath party. This was brutally suppressed in February 1982 in the city of Hama, where 30,000 inhabitants were killed by the Syrian army.[181] This event was Very likely the catalyst that pushed the Brotherhood toward more of a political and social organization and less of a militant organization. The Syrian campaign against the Moslem Brotherhood resulted in displaced refugees from the Syrian Brotherhood being among the first volunteers to fight in Afghanistan and served as added incentive to other national branches of the Brotherhood to assist in the recruiting, training, and movement of volunteers to Afghanistan.[182]

The organization today spans every country where Islam is the dominant religion; from North Africa, the Arabian Peninsula, and Southwest Asia to Indonesia and India. The Brotherhood is also established in the major Western nations of Germany, France, and Great Britain. In the Moslem communities of these countries, the Brotherhood has established Islamic Centers which are suspected to facilitate the movement of extremists throughout North Africa and the West.[183]

Many of the extremist groups are "spin offs" or derivatives of the Moslem Brotherhood. These include the PLO, whose ideology is derived from the principles of the Brotherhood, Hamas and the Palestine Islamic Jihad, Gama'a and Al Jihad in Egypt, Al Nahda in Tunisia, FIS in Algeria, and the NIF in Sudan.[184] These elements separated from the parent organization to pursue violent methods to achieve their goals. Although the Moslem Brotherhood disagrees with the derivative movements in methodology, their goals remain the same.

A roll call of the members of the Moslem Brotherhood would reveal the leadership of nearly every Islamic extremist group in the world. These include Hassan al-Turabi, the Secretary-General of Sudan's NIF; Omar Abdel Rahman, the spiritual mentor of

Egypt's Gama'a and Al Jihad, as well as the mentor of the World Trade Center terrorists; Rashid al-Ghannoushi, leader of Tunisia's al Nahda; Abassi Madani, one of the leaders of Algeria's FIS; and Golbuddin Hekmatyar, leader of Afghanistan's Islamic Party.[185] This membership is the common thread that unites all of these extremist leaders.

The assistance provided to the Islamist extremist groups by the Moslem Brotherhood is primarily financial and logistical. As previously described, the Brotherhood was instrumental in recruiting volunteers for the Afghanistan war and providing a network for transferring men and arms to Afghanistan from the Arab world. Although this network continues to flow to Afghanistan, the return route is much busier, flowing men, arms, and drugs back to bases in Sudan. From Sudan, the flow continues to North Africa, Israel, and the European Islamic Centers for transfer to North Africa and the United States.

Although the Brotherhood does not officially sanction the behavior of extremist groups, the organization clearly has sympathizers in influential positions that use their power and influence to assist their more radical brethren in the pursuit of their goals.

V. CONCLUSION

Implications

The goals of the United States and the Islamic extremists are in conflict. The Islamists desire the removal of Western influence from the Middle East, the establishment of an Islamic republic throughout the lands that once comprised the Islamic empire, and dominance over pricing decisions of Persian Gulf oil.

The affairs of the Middle East will remain a national interest of the United States and the Western world (including Japan and South Korea) as long as their dependence on oil for energy remains high. Stable allies in the area that ensure the unhindered flow of oil are also a national interest, as are access to strategic chokepoints such as the Strait of Hormuz, the Bab el Mandeb, and the Suez Canal. The United States will continue to offer a protective umbrella to the GCC countries that Iran desires to dominate and intimidate.

The threat of nuclear proliferation is a serious implication to the West. The fear of an irrational power that might use a limited number of nuclear weapons to acquire vital national resources, close off chokepoints, or attempt political extortion continues to haunt the West.[186]

The main conventional threat presented by the extremists is Iran. With the acquisition of standoff weapons and diesel submarines, Iran is capable of not only striking the GCC countries, but also possesses the capability to interfere with shipping throughout the Persian Gulf and particularly in the Strait of Hormuz.

Iran has developed the capability to launch forces across the Gulf onto the Arabian Peninsula as was displayed in their "Victory 3" amphibious exercise. The Iranians can sealift one armor brigade in a single lift, and attack with one airborne brigade and four special forces brigades in the initial assault. Although the lift of their Navy is limited, they can sustain and reinforce the initial assault by supplementing the Navy with their 133 ship merchant marine.[187]

A second order conventional threat is the potential takeover of arsenals in states such as Egypt and Algeria. A hostile regime possessing modern weaponry would threaten U.S. shipping and could forcibly deny the Suez Canal to U.S. and allied shipping. The conventional threat posed by Islamist regimes would also destabilize the area by threatening more moderate neighboring regimes. The existing system of states in the region is also at risk. International and regional cooperation are vital to facilitate, trade and counter aggression. Islamist states that withdraw from the world community in this vital region will have a great impact on international law and order and the global economy.

The most serious threat presented by the Islamic extremists is simplistic terrorist type operations - bombings, assassinations, kidnappings, and other acts of violence targeted at government forces or civilians. The network for training and transporting men and materials is well established, making use of diplomatic cover to cross international borders, and using the drug trade to finance more and more of the operations. This spectrum of conflict is most dangerous to us because of the manning, training, and organization of our military. The military is trained to fight conventional opponents where the enemy is identified and separated from the populace. Terrorist operations are conducted by anonymous forces that blend into the civilian population and require patient, diligent police-type work to counter. Within the U.S., we can rely on the capabilities of the FBI to protect us from terrorism, but tend to rely on the military to counter terrorist aggression abroad. We are well equipped to fight the most sophisticated types of conflict but close to powerless to face the type of conflict embodied in terrorist operations. Figure 6 provides a graphic display of our capabilities versus the likelihood of occurrence.

The continued attempts to subvert secular regimes in North Africa present an immediate concern. Algeria is near civil war and in imminent danger of collapse. The possibility is very likely that Algeria will break down into an anarchy where several political-military factions vie for control of the country, similar to Afghanistan.[188] If this level of instability arises in Algeria, it will have a destabilizing effect in Morocco and Tunisia by the flow of refugees and the safe havens and support that will be available to their own Islamist movements from an Islamist Algeria.

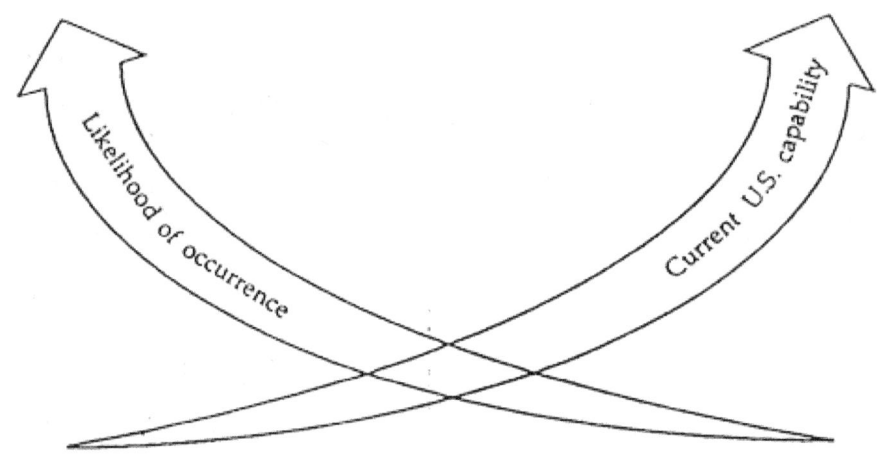

Terrorism   Insurgency   Conventional war   Limited   Strategic war
                                                       nuclear war

Figure 6. U.S. Military Capabilities versus Likelihood of Occurrence[189]

The instability of a fractured Algeria would also have repercussions on Europe, particularly France. European workers living in Algeria, members of the current Algerian ruling party, and other refugees would flow to France, providing a drain upon the French economy.

Egypt faces violence on a daily basis from the Islamist movements that strive to overthrow the Mubarak government. Egypt is the key ally of the United States in North Africa. The loss of this ally, the denial of access to the Suez Canal, and a new threat to Israel by a hostile regime to the south clearly make the fate of Egypt a key interest to the United States.

Although the violence in Egypt is likely to continue, the survival of the Mubarak government is not at high risk. The

extremist movements have only a small base of support within the
population and the 430,000 man armed forces will likely remain
loyal to the regime.[190]

Extremist Organization

This paper has shown that the various Islamic movements are
well organized, share networks, and cooperate to achieve common
goals. However, the various movements are not centrally
controlled and conduct operations independent of the other
national entities.

All of the movements are "home grown"; they have a national
identity based upon a sense of grievance, primarily due to
economic and social conditions. They do share common goals with
other Islamist movements, such as uniform application of the
shari'a throughout the societies of the Middle East and the
unification of all Islamic nations.

The divisions that exist among the Islamic extremists will
limit the degree to which they cooperate. These divisions
include Sunni/Shia, Arab/Persian, nationalism, clan loyalties,
and followers of different schools of thought within the sects
of Islam. Any subordination of one segment to another would be
the equivalent of blasphemy.[191]

Cooperation among the extremists is based upon a quid pro
quo relationship. The cooperation will last only so long as the
interests are compatible and progress is made in achieving the
goals of each group. The example of the support for Gama'a and

Al Jihad in Egypt reveals the interweaving of goals. Gama'a and Al Jihad seek the overthrow of the Mubarak government and the installation of an Islamic state. Iran, in its bid for hegemony in the Persian Gulf, seeks to thwart any attempt by the U.S. to facilitate Egypt exerting a greater role in the Persian Gulf. Thus, Iran provides training and funding to the Egyptian extremist groups to focus the Egyptian government on internal security and away from external commitments. Sudan seeks oil, arms, and funding to attempt to resolve its civil war. These assets are provided by Iran; in return Sudan provides training camps and safe havens for the Egyptian extremists. The Islamic Party of Afghanistan seeks funding, political legitimacy and a network for drug trade. Sudan and Iran provide this in return for the training and combat experience provided in Afghanistan. The common goal that all elements are striving for is the export of the Islamic revolution and the restoration of the Islamic empire.

Recommendations

Nine recommendations are made to meet the threat presented by Islamic extremism. These recommendations are focussed at the underlying sources which tend to breed extremism: economic and social grievances; and the state sponsored support of extremist movements.

1) Threatened countries must focus attention on basic social and economic problems and take measures to alleviate them.

The success of Tunisia and the Gulf nations in combatting extremism reveal the strength of this recommendation. Government efforts to combat poverty and unemployment and provide responsive social services to the poor cut the base of support for the extremists.

2) U.S. assistance to threatened allies must be maintained. We cannot take the attitude of "... letting the flames burn themselves out whenever we are not in danger of catching fire ourselves."[192] We must encourage and aid our allies as they work to improve conditions among their poor and not add to their problems by tying our aid to their conformity to a Western based democracy that their Moslem societies may not support.

3) Institute an embargo of Sudan if support of terrorism is not stopped. U.S. officials predict the Bashir regime would fall in the event of a successful embargo.[193] Their pressing ethnic and economic problems could bring about another change of government or a modification in the stance of the current government to conform to international norms of behavior.

4) Maintain a U.S. presence in the Persian Gulf and the vicinity of our threatened allies. A military presence is necessary to show our resolve to protect our national interests.

5) Apply diplomatic pressure to the GCC countries and Pakistan to cease support of all extremist organizations. Pakistan continues to support the factions in Afghanistan. Private citizens in the GCC support movements throughout the

Middle East. The U.S. must inform these countries of the destabilizing and dangerous behavior of the movements they fund.

6) Apply diplomatic pressure to Egypt, Pakistan, Jordan, and the GCC countries to in turn influence their national branches of the Moslem Brotherhood to cease all manner of support to all extremist organizations.

7) Maintain vigorous diplomatic effort to resolve tension with Iran. The critical vulnerability of Iran is the economy. Debt, high inflation, and high unemployment are problems that the Islamic Republic is proving incapable of correcting. The West may find an opening by arranging assistance in correcting Iran's economic problems in return for an end in Iran's support of terrorism and aggressive actions toward the GCC.

8) Prioritize U.S. intelligence efforts to develop the capability to neutralize the Iranian nuclear program. Our efforts at attempting to control nuclear proliferation in the Middle East and Southwest Asia appears to be of limited success. We cannot afford to be held hostage by a nuclear armed and hostile Iran; we must develop the capability to neutralize the Iranian program at short notice should the contingency arise.

9) Ensure domestic law enforcement and counterterrorism agencies are given maximum freedom of action in maintaining surveillance of potential Islamic extremists. The World Trade Center bombing and the subsequent plots reveal the ruthlessness, effectiveness, and determination of extremist terrorists in exporting their methods to the United-States. Our legal system

must be responsive to the special needs of counterterrorism specialists and allow them latitude in their efforts to preempt domestic terrorism. Our nation has the finest and most advanced investigative arm in the world and we should not handicap their efforts to prevent terrorist operations in this country in the future.

ENDNOTES

1.   Michael C. Hudson, "The Clinton Administration and the Middle East: Squandering the Inheritance", Current History, 93 (February 1994), p. 53.

2.   Charles Krauthammer, "Messianic and Ruthless, Iran Is Flywheel of New Comintern", Richmond Times-Dispatch, 2 January 1993, p. All.

3.   Yossef Bodansky, Target America: Terrorism in the U.S. Today, (New York: Shapolsky Publishers, 1993), p. 151.

4.   Richard W. Bulliet, "The Future of the Islamic Movement", Foreign Affairs, 72 (November - December 1993), p. 41.

5.   Hudson, p. 53.

6.   Robin Wright, Sacred Rage: The Wrath of Militant Islam, (New York: Simon and Schuster, 1986), p. 20.

7.   Ibid.

8.   James A. Bill and Robert Springborg, Politics in the Middle East, (New York: Harper Collins College Publishers, 1994), pp. 54-55.

9.   Ibid.

10. Aims and Principles of the Moslem Brotherhood, Enclosure No. 1 to Dispatch No. 883, Damascus, Syria, 19 December 1947.

11. George J. Church, "Laying Hands on an Unwanted Guest", Time, 142 (12 July 1993), p. 27.

12. Transcript of "Three Days in Beirut", CBS News 60 Minutes, 16 January 1994.

13. Tom Post, "A New Alliance for Terror?", Newsweek, 119 (24 February 1992), p. 32.

14. Francis Robinson, Atlas of the Islamic World Since 1500, (New York: Facts On File, 1982), p. 172.

15. Secretary of Defense Dick Cheney, Defense Strategy for the 1990s: The Regional Defense Strategy, January 1993, p. 3.

16. Ibid., p. 23.

17. Robinson, p. 88.

18. Joseph S. Nye, Jr., "Why the Gulf War Served the National Interest", The Atlantic Monthly, July 1991, p. 54.

19. Robinson, p. 172.

20. Thomas McNaugher, Arms and Oil: U.S. Military Strategy and the Persian Gulf, (Washington, D.C.: The Brookings Institute, 1985), pp. 3-4.

21. Peter G. Peterson, Facing Up: How to Rescue the Economy From Crushing Debt and Restore the American Dream, (New York: Simon and Schuster, 1993), p. 160.

22. Nye, p. 54.

23. Ibid., p. 57.

24. Ibid., p. 56.

25. Kenneth L. Adelman and Norman R. Augustine, The Defense Revolution, (San Francisco: Institute for Contemporary Studies, 1990), p. 78.

26. Michael A. Palmer, "U.S. Must Maintain Mideast Leadership Role", Armed Forces Journal International, February 1993, p. 26.

27. General Joseph P. Hoar, "Central Command's Missions, Responsibilities Continue to Expand: Commander in Chief, U.S. Central Command, to the Senate Armed Services Committee", Defense Issues, 8 (20 April 1993), p. 3.

28. Ibid., p. 13.

29. Louise Lief, "The Battle for Egypt", U.S. News and World Report (USNWR), 115 (19 July 1993), p. 42.

30. Palmer, p. 26.

31. Robert S. Greenberger, "Iran's Economic Problems Could Spark Friction Between U.S. and Allies", The Wall Street Journal, 3 January 1~94, p. A8.

32. Louise Lief, "Iran's New Offensive", USNWR, 112 (30 March 1992), p. 40.

33. Helen Chapin Metz, ed., Iran: A Country Study, (Washington, D.C.: Federal Research Division of the Library of Congress, 1989); p. 155.

34. Tom Masland, "The Threat That Gets Overlooked: Iran", Newsweek, 121 (25 January 1993), p. 43.

35. Edward B. Atkeson, <u>A Military Assessment of the Middle East, 1991-1996</u>, (Carlisle, PA: Strategic Studies Institute, U.S. Army War College, 7 December 1992), p. 35.

36. James Wyllie, "Iran - Quest for Security and Influence", <u>Jane's Intelligence Review</u>, 5 (July 1993), p. 311.

37. Ray Wilkinson, "Springtime in Teheran?", <u>Newsweek</u>, 119 (27 April 1992), p. 38.

38. Richard Z. Chesnoff, "A Little Shopping for Horrors", <u>USNWR</u>, 113 (23 November 1992), p. 52.

39. Bruce W. Nelan, "Diplomacy of Terror", <u>Time</u>, 141 (31 May 1993), p. 47 and Ibid.

40. Wyllie, p. 312.

41. David Dilegge, Intelligence Research Specialist, USMC Intelligence Activity, interview with author at Quantico, VA, 10 February 1994; and Wyllie, p. 312.

42. Atkeson, p. 34.

43. Michael C. Dunn, "Iran's Alarming Military Buildup Transfixes Wary Gulf Neighbors", <u>The Washington Report on Middle East Affairs (TWROMEA)</u>, 11. (October 1992), p. 35; and Wilkinson, p. 38.

44. Ibid.; Lief, "Iran's New Offensive", p. 42; and Wyllie, p. 312.

45. Michael C. Dunn, "More Questions About Iran's Intentions in the Gulf", <u>TWROMEA</u>, 11 (July 1992), p. 31; and Atkeson, p. 36.

46. Chuck Summers, Intelligence Research Specialist, USMC Intelligence Activity, interview with author at Quantico, VA, 9 February 1994.

47. John Kifner, "Khomeini Organizes A New Armed Force", <u>New York Times, 7</u> May 1979, p. Al.

48. Shirleen T. Hunter, <u>Iran After Khomeini</u>, (New York: Praeger Publishers, 1992), p. 51.

49. Ibid., pp. 48-49; and Lief, "Iran's New Offensive", p. 42.

50. Metz, p. 304.

51. Ibid., p. 233.

52. Thomas L. Friedman, From Beirut to Jerusalem, (New York: Farrar Straus Giroux, 1989), p. 505; and Wright, p. 80.

53. Lara Marlowe, "Deep in Kidnapper Country", Time, 138 (19 August 1991), p. 34.

54. Nathan M. Adams, "Iran's Mastermind of World Terrorism", The Reader's Digest, 137 (September 1990), pp. 61-63; and Ibid., p. 22.

55. Wright, p. 88.

56. Richard Z. Chesnoff, "Bad Company in Khartoum", USNWR, 115 (30 August/6 September 1993), p. 45; and "Sudan is Placed on U.S. Terrorism List", U.S. Department of State Dispatch, 4 (23 August 1993), p. 599.

57. Wilhelm Dietl, Holy War, (New York: MacMillan Publishing Company, 1984), p. 293; and Hoar, p. 4.

58. "Toll of Iran-Linked Assassinations Rising in Europe and the Middle East", TWROMEA, 11 (March 1993), p. 39.

59. Louise Lief, "Murder They Wrote: Iran's Web of Terror", USNWR, 111 (16 December 1991), p. 67.

60. Thomas W. Lippman, "White House Sees Iran as Worst 'Outlaw'", The Washington Post, 27 February 1994, p. A31; and Hoar, p. 14.

61. Walter Lacquer and Yonah Alexander, The Terrorism Reader, (New York: Penguin Books, 1987), pp. 331-332.

62. Tim Weiner, "Blowback From the Afghan Battlefield", New York Times Sunday Magazine, 13 March 1994, p. 53.

63. Adam Zagorin, "A House Divided", Foreign Policy, (Fall 1982), p. 116.

64. "Toll of Iran-Linked Assassinations Rising in Europe and the Middle East", p. 39.

65. Benjamin Netanyahu, ed., Terrorism: How the West Can Win, (New York: Farrar Straus Giroux, 1986), p. 33.

66. Summers.

67. Edward Mortimer, Faith and Power: The Politics of Islam, (New York: Random House, 1982), p. 261; and Dietl, p. 198.

68. Helen Chapin Metz, ed., <u>Sudan: A Country Study</u>, (Washington, D.C.: Federal Research Division of the Library of Congress, 1992), pp. 207-219; Dietl, p. 198; and Mortimer, p. 261.

69. Kerry Riley, Intelligence Research Specialist, USMC Intelligence Activity, interview with author at Quantico, VA, 9 February 1994.

70. "'Plots' in Sudan", <u>The Economist Foreign Report</u>, (3 October 1991), p. 3.

71. Raymond Bonner, "Letter From Sudan", <u>The New Yorker</u>, 68 (13 July 1992), p. 74.

72. Ibid., pp. 70 and 82.

73. Marguerite Michaels, "Is Sudan Terrorism's New Best Friend?", <u>Time</u>, 142 (30 August 1993), p. 30; Post, p. 32; and Bodansky, pp.150-151.

74. Bonner, p. 80; and Metz, <u>Sudan: A Country Study</u>, p. xxxi.

75. Metz, <u>Iran: A Country Study</u>, p. 48; and Bodansky, p. 148.

76. Chesnoff, "Bad Company in Khartoum"; and Michaels, p. 30.

77. J. C. Gumucio, "A New Dawn for Islam", <u>World Press Review</u>, 40 (June 1993), p. 19.

78. Mortimer, p. 26.

79. Michaels, p. 30; and Chesnoff, "Bad Company in Khartoum", p. 45.

80. "Deputy Speaker Defects to UK, Speaks on Terrorism", <u>Foreign Broadcast Information Service (FBIS) Daily Report. Near East and South Asia</u>, 24 January 1994.

81. Michael C. Dunn, "Egypt, Algeria, Tunisia Accuse Sudan, as Halaib Dispute Flares Up", <u>TWROMEA</u>, 11 (February 1993), p. 33.

82. Jay Peterzell, "How the Sheikh Got In", <u>Time</u>, 141 (24 May 1993), p. 44.

83. Brian Duffy, "What Kind of Terror Network?", <u>USNWR</u>, 115 (5 July 1993), p. 26; and George J. Church, "The Terror Within", <u>Time</u>, 142 (5 July 1993), p. 22.

84. "Fighting the Holy War", <u>National Review</u>, 45 (19 July 1993), p. 14.

85. Irvin Molotsky, "U.S. Expected To Place Sudan on Terrorist List", New York Times, 17 August 1993, p. B3.

86. "Starvation in a Fruitful Land", Time, 132 (5 December 1988), p. 43.

87. Metz, Sudan: A Country Study, pp. xxx and xxxi.

88. Louise Lief, "Starvation as a Political Weapon", USNWR, 106 (6 February 1989), p. 34.

89. "Conflict Between Egypt and Sudan?", The Economist Foreign Report, 11 June 1992, p. 7.

90. Todd Shields, "Maestros of Mayhem", USNWR, 115 (30 August/6 September 1993), p. 43.

91. Jeffrey Bartholet, "Hidden Horrors in Sudan", Newsweek, 120 (12 October 1992), p. 49.

92. Metz, Sudan: A Country Study, p. xxxiii.

93. "Sudan Launches Offensive Against Southern Rebels", The Washington Post, 6 February 1994, p. A24; and Keith B. Richburg, "Sudan Launches Offensive Against Rebels", The Washington Post, 8 February 1994, p. A14.

94. Bonner, p. 76.

95. Aims and Principles of the Moslem Brotherhood.

96. William R. Doerner, "Rebels With Too Many Causes", Time, 133 (27 February 1989), p. 39; and Mary Anne Weaver, "The Trail of the Sheikh", The New Yorker, 69 (12 April 1993), p. 79.

97. Weiner, p. 54.

98. Ibid., p. 53.

99. Anthony Davis, "Foreign Combatants in Afghanistan", Jane's Intelligence Review, 5 (July 1993), p. 329.

100. Bodansky, p. 141.

101. Weiner, p. 53.

102. Ibid., p. 54 and Weaver, p. 79.

103. "Al-Turabi Mediation to Continue at Khartoum Forum", FBIS Daily Report. Near East and South Asia, 26 November 1993, p. 53.

104. Brian Duffy and Peter Corey, "What Goes Around", <u>USNWR</u>, 115 (30 August/6 September 1993), P. 48.

105. Molly Moore, "Missile Buyback Stumbles", <u>The Washington Post</u>, 7 March 1994, p. Al.

106. Ibid.

107. "Shiekh Urges Attacks on U.S. Army, Transcripts of Tapes Show", <u>New York Times</u>, 7 March 1994, p. B4.

108. Weiner, pp. 53-54.

109. Dietl, pp. 289-292.

110. Rouhollah K. Ramazani, <u>Revolutionary Iran</u>, (Baltimore, MD: The John Hopkins University Press, 1988), pp. 40-41.

111. Wright, pp. 114-119 and Ibid., pp. 48-52.

112. Wright, p. 112 and Ramazani, pp. 42-48.

113. Hoar, p. 11.

114. Bruce W. Nelan, "The Dark Side of Islam", <u>Time</u>, 142 (4 October 1993), p. 62.

115. Weaver, pp. 76 and 86.

116. Ibid., pp. 78-79.

117. "The Afghan Connection", <u>Time</u>, 142 (4 October 1993), p. 64 and James Wyllie, "Egypt - A State in Jeopardy", <u>Jane's Intelligence Review</u>, 6 (January 1994), p. 29.

118. Edward A. Gargan, "Where Arab Militants Train and Wait", <u>New York Times</u>; 11 August 1993, p. A8.

119. Ibid. and Bodansky, p. 141.

120. Weiner, p. 54; Weaver, p. 79; and "The Afghan Connection".

121. Weaver, p. 78.

122. Bruce W. Nelan, "Bombs in the Name of Allah", <u>Time</u>, 142 (30 August 1993), p. 28 and Jeffrey Bartholet, "A Wave of Terror All Their Own", <u>Newsweek</u>, 122 (30 August 1993), p. 41.

123. Judith Miller, "Bloody Sheikh", <u>The New Republic</u>, 208 (29 March 1993), p. 19.

124. Joel Gordon, "Political Opposition in Egypt", Current History, 89 (February 1990), p. 79 and Jeffrey L. Sheler, "Scouring the Koran For Fighting Words", USNWR, 115 (16 August 1993), p. 52.

125. Weaver, p. 86.

126. "5 Egyptian Christians Killed; Muslim Radicals Are Blamed", The Washington Post, 13 March 1994, p. A27.

127. Jill Smolowe, "A Voice of Holy War", Time, 141 (15 March 1993), p. 34.

128. Bill Turque, "An Iranian Connection?", Newsweek, 121 (22 March 1993), p. 33.

129. Lara Marlowe, "Faith's Fearsome Sword", Time, 143 (7 February 1994), p. 48.

130. Jill Smolowe, "An Alarming No Vote", Time, 139 (13 January 1992), p. 28.

131. Jill Smolowe, "A Prelude to Civil War?", Time, 139 (27 January 1992), p. 30.

132. Greg and Laudia Chouat Noakes, "Facing Uncertain Future and Violent Present, Algerians Turn to Idealized Past", TWROMEA, 11 (February 1993), p. 35.

133. Marlowe, p. 49.

134. Russell Watson, "An Army of Eternal Victims", Newsweek, 121 (15 March 1993), p. 34 and Weiner, p. 54.

135. Jon D. Hull, "Farewell to Moderation", Time, 137 (7 January 1991), p. 65.

136. Marguerite Michaels, "Hamas: Dying for Israel's Destruction", Time, 142 (13 September 1993), p. 38.

137. Bulliet, p. 41.

138. Hull and Michaels, "Hamas: Dying for Israel's Destruction".

139. Richard Z. Chesnoff, "Fundamentalist Fears", USNWR, 114 (11 January 1993), p. 30.

140. Patterns of Global Terrorism, 1992, United States Department of State, April 1993, pp. 3 and 38.

141. Fouad Ajami, "Inside the Mind of a Movement", USNWR, 107 (14 August 1989), p. 28.

142. <u>Patterns of Global Terrorism. 1992</u>, p. 19.

143. Peter Ford, "Hizbollah Forces Lob New Threats at Israel", <u>Christian Science Monitor</u>, 14 February 1994, p. 4.

144. "Future Hezbollah-Hamas Operations Proposed", <u>FBIS Daily Report, Near East and South Asia</u>, 6 January 1994.

145. "U.S. Sees Iranian Role in Buenos Aires Blast", <u>New York Times</u>, 9 May 1992, p. A3.

146. John L. Esposito, "Political Islam: Beyond the Green Menace", <u>Current History</u>, 93 (January 1994), p. 21.

147. Mary C. Wilson, "Jordan: Bread, Freedom or Both?", <u>Current History</u>, 93 (February 1994), p. 88.

148. <u>Patterns of Global Terrorism, 1992</u>, p. 18.

149. George J. Mirsky, "Central Asia's Emergence", <u>Current History</u>, 91 (October 1992), p. 334.

150. Haroon Siddiqui, "The Scramble for Central Asia", <u>World Press Review</u>, 39 (July 1992), pp. 9 and 10.

151. "Iran Takes Aim at Tajikistan", <u>The Economist Foreign Report</u>, 30 April 1992, pp. 4 and 5; Hoar, p. 4; and Weiner, p. 54.

152. "Pointers", <u>The Economist Foreign Report</u>, 12 November 1992.

153. Siddiqui, p. 9.

154. Chesnoff, "Bad Company in Khartoum"; and interview with Riley.

155. Mary Anne Fitzgerald, "Ethnic Divisions Plague Ethiopia", <u>The Washington Times</u>, 3 February 1994, p. A13.

156. "Deputy Speaker Defects to UK, Speaks on Terrorism", <u>FBIS-NES-94-015</u>.

157. "Islam is Spreading in East Africa", <u>The Economist Foreign Report</u>, 4 June 1992, p. 7.

158. James Wyllie, "Yemen - On the Brink", <u>Jane's Intelligence Review</u>, 6 (March 1994), pp. 130-131.

159. "Muslim Fundamentalism in Africa", <u>The Economist Foreign Report</u>, 4 February 1993, pp. 4 and 5; and "Islam is Spreading in East Africa".

160. Kent H. Butts, "The DoD Role in African Policy", _Parameters_, XXIII (Winter 1993-1994), p. 60.

161. Margaret A. Jacobs, "Trade Center Convictions May Bring Deals", _The Wall Street Journal_, 7 March 1994, p. B7.

162. George J. Church, "Laying Hands on an Unwanted Guest", p. 27.

163. Bill Turque, "A Trail to the Jihad Office", _Newsweek_, 121 (29 March 1993), p. 38.

164. Ralph Blumenthal, "Some Cited in Bomb Plot Are Linked to Drug Sales", _New York Times_, 20 July 1993, p. B3.

165. Weiner, pp. 54-55.

166. George J. Church, "Snared in the Terrorist Web", _Time_, 142 (6 September 1993), p. 30.

167. Weaver, p. 73.

168. Duffy, p. 26.

169. Ibid.

170. Stephen Lee Myers, "Man in New Jersey is Charged in Plot to Kill Mubarak", _New York Times_, 18 July 1993, p. C1.

171. Ralph Blumenthal, "Plot to Abduct Nixon to Free Blast Suspects", _New York Times_, 6 September 1993, p. J17.

172. Richard Z. Chesnoff, "Between Bombers and Believers", _USNWR_, 115 (20 September 1993), p. 34.

173. Chris Hedges, "Egyptian Says Confession Links Iran to Bombing of Trade Center", _New York Times_, 16 July 1993, p. A1.

174. Rachel Ehrenfeld, "Follow the Money", _National Review_, 45 (1 November 1993), p. 52.

175. Blumenthal, "Some Cited in Bomb Plot Are Linked to Drug Sales".

176. "Trade Center Mysteries Deepen", _New York Times_, 15 November 1993, p. Bi.

177. "Fighting the Unholy War".

178. Molotsky.

179. David van Biema, "So Glad to See You", _Time_, 141 (5 April 1993), p. 33.

180. Mortimer, pp. 256-258.

181. Dietl, pp. 133-140.

182. Davis, pp. 329-330.

183. Ibid.

184. Tom Masland, "Building an Enemy", _Newsweek_, 121 (15 February 1993), p. 29 and Mortimer, p. 259.

185. Judith Miller, "The Challenge of Radical Islam", _Foreign Affairs_, 72 (Spring 1993), p. 43.

186. Adelman and Augustine, p. 58.

187. Atkeson, pp. 70 and 71.

188. Bruce Riedel, National Intelligence Officer, Near East and South Asia, comments at the Central Intelligence Agency, Langley, VA, 21 March 1994.

189. Adelman and Augustine, p. 58.

190. Riedel.

191. Summers.

192. Ralph Peters, "Vanity and the Bonfire of the 'Isms'", _Parameters_, XXIII (Autumn 1993), p. 50.

193. Riley.

BIBLIOGRAPHY

1. Adams, Nathan M. "Iran's Mastermind of World Terrorism." The Reader's Digest, 137 (September 1990).

2. Adelman, Kenneth L. and Augustine, Norman R. The Defense Revolution. San Francisco: Institute for Contemporary Studies, 1990.

3. "The Afghan Connection." Time, 142 (4 October 1993).

4. Ahmed, Makram Muhammed. "Algeria at the Brink." World Press Review, 38 (September 1991).

5. Aims and Principles of the Moslem Brotherhood. Enclosure No. 1 to Dispatch No. 883, Damascus, Syria, 19 December 1947.

6. Ajami, Fouad. "Inside the Mind of a Movement." U.S. News and World Report (USNWR), 107 (14 August 1989).

7. "Al-Turabi Mediation to Continue at Khartoum Forum." Foreign Broadcast Information Service (FBIS) Daily Report, Near East and South Asia, 26 November 1993.

8. Atkeson, Edward B. A Military Assessment of the Middle East, 1991-1996. Carlisle, PA: Strategic Studies Institute, U.S. Army War College, 7 December 1992.

9. Bartholet, Jeffrey. "Hidden Horrors in Sudan." Newsweek, 120 (12 October 1992)

10. Bartholet, Jeffrey. "A Wave of Terror All their Own." Newsweek, 122 (30 August 1993).

11. Becker, Jillian. The PLO. New York: St. Martin's Press, 1984.

12. Behar, Richard. "The Secret Life of Mahmud the Red." Time, 142 (4 October 1993)

13. Bill, James A. and Springborg, Robert. Politics in the Middle East. New York: Harper Collins College Publishers, 1994.

14. Blumenthal, Ralph. "Plot to Abduct Nixon to Free Blast Suspects." New York Times, 6 September 1993.

15. Blumenthal, Ralph. "Some Cited in Bomb Plot Are Linked to Drug Sales." New York Times, 20 July 1993.

16. Bodansky, Yossef. Target America: Terrorism in the U.S. Today. New York: Shapolsky Publishers, 1993.

17. Bonner, Raymond. "Letter From Sudan." The New Yorker, 68 (13 July 1992)

18. Bremer III, L. Paul. "With Assad, Talk About Terrorism." The Wall Street Journal, 14 January 1994.

19. Bulliet, Richard W. "The Future of the Islamic Movement." Foreign Affairs, 72 (November - December 1993).

20. Butts, Kent H. "The DoD Role in African Policy." Parameters, XXIII (Winter 1993-1994).

21. Cheney, Dick, Secretary of Defense. Defense Strategy for the 1990s: The Regional Defense Strategy, January 1993.

22. Chesnoff, Richard Z. "Bad Company in Khartoum." USNWR, 115 (30 August/6 September 1993).

23. Chesnoff, Richard Z. "Between Bombers and Believers." USNWR, 115 (20 September 1993).

24. Chesnoff, Richard Z. "Fundamentalist Fears." USNWR, 114 (11 January 1993).

25. Chesnoff, Richard Z. "A Little Shopping for Horrors." USNWR, 113 (23 November 1992).

26. Church, George J. "Laying Hands on an Unwanted Guest." Time, 142 (12 July 1993)

27. Church, George J. "Snared in the Terrorist Web" Time, 142 (6 September 1993).

28. Church, George J. "The Terror Within." Time, 142 (5 July 1993)

29. "Conflict Between Egypt and Sudan?" The Economist Foreign Report, 11 June 1992.

30. Davis, Anthony. "Foreign Combatants in Afghanistan." Jane's Intelligence Review, 5 (July 1993).

31. "Deputy Speaker Defects to UK, Speaks On Terrorism." FBIS-NES-94-015, 24 January 1994.

32. "Deputy Speaker Defects, Details Foreign Terrorist Training." JPRS-TOT-94-004, 31 January 1994.

33. Desmond, Edward W. "A Revolution Loses Its Zeal." Time,137
        (6 May 1991).

34. Dietl, Wilhelm. Holy War. New York: MacMillan Publishing
        Company, 1984.

35. Dilegge, David, Intelligence Research Specialist, USMC
        Intelligence Activity. Interview with author at
        Quantico, VA, 10 February 1994.

36. Dini, Massimo. "The Growing Influence of God's Fanatics."
        World Press Review, 39 (March 1992).

37. Doerner, William R. "Rebels With Too Many Causes." Time,
        133 (27 February 1989).

38. Duffy, Brian and Corey, Peter. "What Goes Around." USNWR,
        115 (30 August/6 September 1993)

39. Duffy, Brian. "What Kind of Terror Network?", USNWR, 115 (5
        July 1993)

40. Dunn, Michael C. "Egypt, Algeria, Tunisia Accuse Sudan, as
        Halaib Dispute Flares Up." The Washington Report on
        Middle East Affairs (TWROMEA), 11 (February 1993).

41. Dunn, Michael C. "Iran's Alarming Military Buildup
        Transfixes Wary Gulf Neighbors." TWROMEA, 11 (October
        1992)

42. Dunn, Michael C. "More Questions About Iran's Intentions in
        the Gulf", TWROMEA, 11 (July 1992).

43. "An Early Morning Coup." Time, 134 (10 July 1989).

44.   Ehrenfeld, Rachel. "Follow the Money." National Review, 45
        (1 November 1993).

45. Esposito, John L. "Political Islam: Beyond the Green
        Menace." Current History, 93 (January 1994).

46. "Fighting the Unholy War." National Review, 45 (19 July
        1993)

47. Fitzgerald, Mary Anne. "Ethnic Divisions Plague Ethiopia."
        The Washington Times, 3 February 1994.

48. "5 Egyptian Christians Killed; Muslim Radicals Are Blamed."
        The Washington Post, 13 March 1994.

49. Ford, Peter. "Hizbullah Forces Lob New Threats at Israel."
        Christian Science Monitor, 14 February 1994.

50. Friedman, Thomas L. From Beirut to Jerusalem. New York: Farrar Straus Giroux, 1989.

51. "Future Hezbollah-Hamas Operations Proposed." FBIS Daily Report, Near East and South Asia, 6 January 1994.

52. Garcia, Guy D. "Where Hatred Begets Hatred." Time, 136 (19 November 1990).

53. Gargan, Edward A. "Where Arab Militants Train and Wait." New York Times, 11 August 1993.

54. Georgy, Michael. "Egyptian Militants Vow Attacks on Americans. "New York Times, 5 March 1994.

55. Gordon, Joel. "Political Opposition in Egypt." Current History, 89 (February 1990).

54. Greenberger, Robert S. "Iran's Economic Problems Could Spark Friction Between U.S. and Allies." The Wall Street Journal, 3 January 1994.

55. Gumucio, J. C. "A New Dawn for Islam." World Press Review, 40 (June 1993)

56. Hadar, Leon T. "What Green Peril?" Foreign Affairs, 72 (Spring 1993)

57. Hedges, Chris. "Egyptian Says Confession Links Iran to Bombing of Trade Center." New York Times, 16 July 1993.

58. Helevy, David and Livingstone, Neil C. "An American Soldier's Death Becomes a Pawn in a Terrorist Power Struggle." USNWR, 107 (23 October 1989).

59. Hoar, Joseph P., General, Commander in Chief, U.S. Central Command. "Central Command's Missions, Responsibilities Continue to Expand: Commander in Chief, U.S. Central Command, to the Senate Armed Services Committee." Defense Issues, 8 (20 April 1993)

60. Hudson, Michael C. "The Clinton Administration and the Middle east: Squandering the Inheritance." Current History, 93 (February 1994).

61. Hull, Jon D. "Farewell to Moderation." Time, 137 (7 January 1991).

62. Hunter, Shirleen T. Iran After Khomeini. New York: Praeger Publishers, 1992.

63. "The Immigrants." The New Republic, 208 (19 April 1993).

64. "In Sudan's Beirut Embassy." The Economist Foreign Report, 1 July 1993.

65. "Interior Minister on Security Methods, Afghan Returnees." JPRS-TOT-93-019-L, 18 May 1993.

66. "Iran Takes Aim at Tajikistan." The Economist Foreign Report, 30 April 1992.

67. "Iran to Acquire 30 Russian Helicopters." FBIS Daily Report - Near East and South Asia, 26 November 1993.

68. "Islam is Spreading in East Africa." The Economist Foreign Report, 4 June 1992.

69. Jacobs, Margaret A. "Trade Center Convictions May Bring Deals." The Wall Street Journal, 7 March 1994.

70. Jansen, Johannes G. The Neglected Duty: The Creed of Sadat's Assassins and Islamic Resurgence in the Middle East. New York: Macmillan, 1986.

71. Kifner, John. "Khomeini Organizes A New Armed Force." New York Times, 7 May 1979.

72. Kramer, Martin. "Islam and the West (Including Manhattan)." Commentary, October 1993.

73. Kramer, Martin.) "Musawi's Game." The New Republic, 206 (23 March 1992).

74. Krauthammer, Charles. "Messianic and Ruthless, Iran Is Flywheel of New Comintern." Richmond Times-Dispatch, 2 January 1993.

75. Lacquer, Walter and Alexander, Yonah. The Terrorism Reader. New York: Penguin Books, 1987.

76. Levine Steve. "Perry Seeks Security Pact For Ex-Soviet Republics." The Washington Post, 20 March 1994.

77. Lewis, Bernard. "The Roots of Muslim Rage." The Atlantic Monthly, September 1990.

78. Lief, Louise. "The Battle for Egypt." USNWR, 115 (19 July 1993).

79. Lief, Louise. "Iran's New Offensive." USNWR, 112 (30 March 1992).

80. Lief, Louise. "Murder They Wrote: Iran's Web of Terror." USNWR, 111 (16 December 1991).

81. Lief, Louise. "Starvation as a Political Weapon." <u>USNWR</u>, 106 (6 February 1989).

82. Lippman, Thomas W. "White House Sees Iran as Worst 'Outlaw'." <u>The Washington Post</u>, 27 February 1994.

83. Manegold, C.S. "Teheran and Moscow: Islamic Threat?" <u>Newsweek</u>, 115 (29 January 1992).

84. Marlowe, Lara. "Deep in Kidnapper Country." <u>Time</u>, 138 (19 August 1991).

85. Marlowe, Lara. "Faith's Fearsome Sword." <u>Time</u>, 143 (7 February 1994).

86. Masland, Tom. "Building An Enemy." <u>Newsweek</u>, 121 (15 February 1993).

87. Masland, Tom. "The Threat That Gets Overlooked: Iran." <u>Newsweek</u>, 121 (25 January 1993).

88. McNaugher, Thomas. <u>Arms and Oil: U.S. Military Strategy and the Persian Gulf</u>. Washington, D.C.: The Brookings Institute, 1985.

89. Metz, Helen Chapin, ed. <u>Iran: A Country Study</u>. Washington, D.C.:   Federal Research Division of the Library of Congress, 1989.

90. Metz, Helen Chapin, ed. <u>Sudan: A Country Study</u>. Washington, D.C.: Federal Research Division of the Library of Congress, 1992.

91. Michaels, Marguerite. "Hamas: Dying for Israel's Destruction." <u>Time</u>, 142 (13 September 1993).

92. Michaels, Marguerite. "Is Sudan Terrorism's New Best Friend?" <u>Time</u>, 142 (30 August 1993)

93. Miller, Judith. "Bloody Sheikh." <u>The New Republic</u>, 208 (29 March 1993)

94. Miller, Judith. "The Challenge of Radical Islam." <u>Foreign Affairs</u>, 72 (Spring 1993)

95. Mirsky, George J. "Central Asia's Emergence." <u>Current History</u>, 91 (October 1992).

96. Molotsky, Irvin. "U.S. Expected To Place Sudan on Terrorist List." <u>New York Times</u>, 17 August 1993.

97.   Moore, Molly. "Missile Buyback Stumbles." The Washington
          Post, 7 March 1994.

98.   Mortimer, Edward. Faith and Power: The Politics of Islam.
          New York: Random House, 1982).

99.   Murphy, Caryle. "Egypt: An Uneasy Portent of Change."
          Current History, 93 (February 1994).

100. Muslih, Muhammed. "Jericho and Its Meaning: A New Strategy
          for the Palestinians." Current History, 93 (February
          1994).

101. "Muslim Brotherhood Official on 'Tyrannical Regime'."FBIS-
          NES-94-009, 13 January 1994.

102. "Muslim Fundamentalism in Africa." The Economist Foreign
          Report, 4 February 1993.

103. Myers, Stephen Lee. "Man in New Jersey is Charged in Plot
          to Kill Mubarak." New York Times, 18 July 1993.

104. National Security Strategy of the United States, The White
          House, January 1993.

105. Nelan, Bruce W. "Bombs in the Name of Allah." Time, 142
          (30 August 1993)

106. Nelan, Bruce W. "The Dark Side of Islam." Time, 142
          (4 October 1993)

107. Nelan, Bruce W. "Diplomacy of Terror." Time, 141
          (31 May 1993)

108. Nelan, Bruce W. "Hamas and the Heartland." Time, 141
          (15 February 1993).

109. Nelan, Bruce W. "Trouble on the Nile." Time, 141
          (12 April 1993)

110. Netanyahu, Benjamin, ed. Terrorism: How the West Can Win.
          New York: Farrar Straus Giroux, 1986.

111. "Nine Police Killed in 24 November Ambush." FBIS Daily
          Report - Near East and South Asia, 26 November 1993.

112. Noakes, Greg and Laudia Chouat. "Facing Uncertain Future
          and Violent Present, Algerians Turn to Idealized
          Past." TWROMEA, 11 (February 1993).

113. Norton, Augustus Richard. "The Future of Civil Society in the Middle East." The Middle East Journal, 47 (Spring 1993)

114. Nye, Joseph S., Jr. "Why the Gulf War Served the National Interest." The Atlantic Monthly, July 1991.

115. Parmelee, Jennifer. "Radicals Gain Strength in Horn of Africa." The Washington Post, 5 January 1994.

116. Palmer, Michael A. "US Must Maintain Mideast Leadership Role", Armed Forces Journal International, February 1993.

117. Patterns of Global Terrorism, 1992, United States Department of State, April 1993.

118. Peters, Ralph. "Vanity and the Bonfire of the 'Isms'." Parameters, XXIII (Autumn 1993).

119. Peterson, Peter G. Facing Up: How to Rescue the Economy From Crushing Debt and Restore the American Dream. New York: Simon and Schuster, 1993.

120. Peterzell, Jay. "How the Sheikh Got In." Time, 141 (24 May 1993).

121. "Pointers." The Economist Foreign Report, 12 November 1992.

122. "'Plots' in Sudan." The Economist Foreign Report, 3 October 1991.

123. Post, Tom. "A New Alliance for Terror?" Newsweek, 119 (24 February 1992).

124. Ramazani, Rouhollah K. Revolutionary Iran. Baltimore, MD: The John Hopkins University Press, 1988.

125. Rashad, Ahmad J. "Hamas: The History of the Islamic Opposition Movement in Palestine." TWROMEA, XI (March 1993)

126. Richburg, Keith B. "Sudan Launches Offensive Against Rebels", The Washington Post, 8 February 1994.

127. Riedel, Bruce, National Intelligence Officer, Near East and South Asia. Comments at the Central Intelligence Agency, Langley, VA, 21 March 1994.

128. Riley, Kerry, Intelligence Research Specialist, USMC
        Intelligence Activity. Interview with the author at
        Quantico, VA, 9 February 1994.

129. Robinson, Francis. Atlas of the Islamic World Since 1500.
        New York: Facts On File, 1982.

130. Said, Edward W. "Arabs and Americans." Columbia, Spring
        1993.

131. Sheler, Jeffery L. "Scouring the Koran for Fighting Words."
        USNWR, 115 (16 August 1993)

132. "Sheikh Urges Attacks on U.S. Army, Transcripts of Tapes
        Show." New York Times, 7 March 1994.

133. Shields, Todd. "Maestros of Mayhem." USNWR, 115
        (30 August/6 September 1993).

134. "Shi'ite Against Shi'ite." Time, 131 (23 May 1988).

135. Shirley, Edward G. "Not Fanatics, and Not Friends." The
        Atlantic Monthly, December 1993.

136. Siddiqui, Haroon. "The Scramble for Central Asia." World
        Press Review, 39 (July 1992).

137. Smolowe, Jill. "An Alarming No Vote." Time, 139
        (13 January 1992).

138. Smolowe, Jill. "A Prelude To Civil War?" Time, 139
        (27 January 1992).

139. Smolowe, Jill. "Vengeance Is Mine." Time, 139
        (2 March 1992)

140. Smolowe, Jill. "A Voice of Holy War." Time, 141
        (15 March 1993)

141. "Starvation in a Fruitful Land." Time, 132
        (5 December 1988).

142. Sterling, Claire. The Terror Network. New York: The
        Reader's Digest Press, 1981.

143. "Sudan is Placed on U.S. Terrorism List." U.S. Department
        of State Dispatch, 4 (23 August 1993).

144. "Sudan Launches Offensive Against Southern Rebels." The
        Washington Post, 6 February 1994.

145. Summers, Chuck, Intelligence Research Specialist, USMC Intelligence Activity. Interview with the author at Quantico, VA, 9 February 1994.

146. Thomas, Pierre and Lippman, Thomas W. "U.S. Steps Up Efforts To Combat Terrorism." The Washington Post, 7 November 1993.

147. "Three Days in Beirut", CBS News 60 Minutes, Transcript. 16 January 1994.

148. "Toll of Iran-Linked Assassinations Rising in Europe and the Middle East." TWROMEA, 11 (March 1993).

149. "Trade Center Mysteries Deepen." New York Times, 15 November 1993.

150. Turque, Bill. "An Iranian Connection?" Newsweek, 121 (22 March 1993)

151. Turque, Bill. "A Trail to the Jihad Office." Newsweek, 121 (29 March 1993)

152. "U.S. Sees Iranian Role in Buenos Aires Blast." New York Times, 9 May 1992.

153. van Biema, David. "So Glad to See You." Time, 141 (5 April 1993)

154. Voll, John O. "Political Crisis in Sudan." Current History, 89 (April 1990)

155. Wald, Matthew L. "How Does the World Look Through the Eyes of Aspiring Terrorists?" New York Times, 6 March 1994.

156. Watson, Russell. "An Army of Eternal Victims." Newsweek, 121 (15 March 1993)

157. Weaver, Mary Anne. "The Trail of the Sheikh." The New Yorker, 69 (12 April 1993)

158. Weiner, Tire. "Blowback From the Afghan Battlefield." New York Times Sunday Magazine, 13 March 1994.

159. West, J. Robinson. "America's Addiction to Foreign Oil." The Washington Post, 8 June 1992.

160. Wilkinson, Ray. "Springtime in Teheran?" Newsweek, 119 (27 April 1992)

161. Wilkinson, Ray. "A 'Wind' Turns in Algeria." Newsweek, 117 (17 June 1991)

162. Wilson, Mary C. "Jordan: Bread, Freedom or Both?" Current
      History, 93 (February 1994).

163. Wright, Robin. Sacred Rage: The Wrath of Militant Islam.
      New York: Simon and Schuster, 1986.

164. Wyllie, James. "Egypt - A State in Jeopardy." Jane's
      Intelligence Review, 6 (January 1994).

165. Wyllie, James. "Iran - Quest for Security and Influence."
      Jane's Intelligence Review, 5 (July 1993).

166. Wyllie, James. "Yemen - On the Brink." Jane's Intelligence
      Review, 6 (March 1994).

167. Zagorin, Adam.) "A House Divided." Foreign Policy,
      (Fall 1982).

168. Zuckerman, Mortimer. "Beware of Religious Stalinists.
      "USNWR, 114 (22 March 1993)